Grow Your Own Groceries

Visit our How To Website at www.howto.co.uk

At www.howto.co.uk you can engage in conversation with our authors – all of whom have 'been there and done that' in their specialist fields. You can get access to special offers and additional content but most importantly you will be able to engage with, and become a part of, a wide and growing community of people just like yourself.

At www.howto.co.uk you'll be able to talk and share tips with people who have similar interests and are facing similar challenges in their lives. People who, just like you, have the desire to change their lives for the better – be it through moving to a new country, starting a new business, growing their own vegetables, or writing a novel.

At www.howto.co.uk you'll find the support and encouragement you need to help make your aspirations a reality.

You can to direct to www.grow-your-own-groceries.co.uk which is part of the How To site.

How To Books strives to present authentic, inspiring, practical information in their books. Now, when you buy a title from **How To Books,** you get even more than just words on a page.

Grow Your Own Groceries

HOW TO FEED YOUR FAMILY
FROM YOUR OWN BACK GARDEN

Linda Gray

SPRING HILL

Published by Spring Hill

Spring Hill is an imprint of How To Books Ltd
Spring Hill House, Spring Hill Road,
Begbroke, Oxford, OX5 1RX, United Kingdom
Tel: (01865) 375794 Fax: (01865) 379162
info@howtobooks.co.uk
www.howtobooks.co.uk

How To Books greatly reduce the carbon footprint of their books by sourcing their typesetting
and printing in the UK.

First edition 2009
Reprinted 2009

British Library Cataloguing in Publication Data
A catalogue record for this book is available from the British Library

ISBN: 978 1 905862 31 3

Produced for How To Books by Deer Park Productions, Tavistock
Typeset by TW Typesetting, Plymouth, Devon
Printed and bound by Bell & Bain Ltd, Glasgow

NOTE: The material contained in this book is set out in good faith for general guidance and
no liability can be accepted for loss or expense incurred as a result of relying in particular
circumstances on statements made in this book. Laws and regulations may be complex and
liable to change, and readers should check the current position with the relevant authorities
before making personal arrangements.

CONTENTS

CONTENTS

INTRODUCTION

Producing your own food and other household groceries is not only extremely rewarding but, in times of economic and environment changes, a must!

Gardening has, until recent years, been a way of life and a necessary commitment if families were to survive and grow. Nature provides everything the human body requires to survive, and cultivating some of those natural products in our own back garden will not only produce the best food on the planet for our loved ones, it is also economical and environmentally friendly.

Chemicals don't have to be used to produce perfectly shaped strawberries, petrol is not required to drive into your back garden to collect your food and, not only that, as you are exercising and getting a dose of fresh air every day, gym subscriptions and doctors visits will be a thing of the past.

Many crops can be produced in a relatively small space with a little pre-planning and organising. And many of these crops can be employed in different ways. Herbs are not only perfect for collecting brownie points for your culinary skills, they can also treat minor ailments and prevent colds and flu. Rather than getting a cold virus and passing it round and round the household, refuse to allow it into the house in the first place, by keeping healthy and strong. No more vitamin supplements or cold remedies to buy!

Grow Your Own Groceries provides all the information you need to keep your family and friends healthy and enjoying life to the full. Gardening is more than a hobby, it's a way of life and needn't mean back ache and boring garden chores. Even without a garden, many plants can be grown in containers, on a balcony and indoors.

Get those wellies on and produce the best groceries in the world for your family and friends – and keep fit and healthy while you're doing it. *Grow Your Own Groceries* will reduce your shopping bill, remove the supermarket stress, and take you and your family into a healthier future.

CHAPTER 1

THE SALAD BOWL

A bowl of mixed salad is one of the healthiest, easiest and tastiest meals you can prepare for you and your family. Kids don't always appreciate green leafy vegetables, but chopped lettuce stirred into a bowl of colourful peppers and tomatoes always goes down a treat!

Growing salad ingredients couldn't be easier and many can be grown indoors, in a conservatory or even a window box, as well as outside in a traditional garden. If you have a conservatory or greenhouse, salad can be grown almost all year round – although, as it's eaten raw and often cold straight from the fridge, other veggies from the garden can take over during the cooler months of the year. Eating seasonally is a good rule of thumb when balancing a healthy diet.

This chapter covers five main ingredients of a nutritious and delicious salad bowl:

- tomatoes
- lettuce

- cucumber

- peppers

- onions.

There are many other vegetables you can add as and when you have them available:

- carrots – grated or finely sliced

- garlic – crushed or finely chopped

- *mange tout* – whole or cut in half

- fresh peas or beans – cooked and then cooled

- herbs and edible flowers

- nuts and seeds.

Prepare your salad as close to meal time as possible. As soon as you start cutting vegetables, they begin to lose some of their vitamin content. However, picking your salad from the garden in the afternoon and eating it in the evening is a lot better than buying tired, old looking vegetables from the supermarket. And your garden fresh and (hopefully) organic salad will taste a whole lot better than anything you can possibly buy.

If your little darlings refuse to eat anything that doesn't come out of a packet, you could try tipping the tomatoes into a freezer bag on the quiet and then make a big deal about getting them out of the fridge later. Or even better, get them involved in the garden.

TOMATOES

About tomatoes

There is evidence that the Incan civilization grew tomatoes as a food crop but over the centuries the tomato was grown as an ornamental plant as the fruits were thought to be poisonous.

By the early nineteenth century the tomato was once again considered a worthy food crop and businessmen used to eat tomatoes in public places to prove the fruit was in fact edible and could be safely consumed. The earliest recorded tomato ketchup recipe was developed in 1818.

Because tomato plants are self-pollinating, they tend not to change the components of their particular variety very much, which means we have many heirloom varieties available today, as well as many new hybrids in all sorts of shapes and colours.

Properties of tomatoes

Recent scientific experiments indicate that tomatoes, especially cooked ones, can help eliminate free radicals from the body, so reducing the risk of certain cancers.

Tomatoes contain significant amounts of vitamins A, B1, B2, B6 and vitamin C. They also contain fibre and a medium-sized tomato will only add around 20 calories to your daily calorie count.

Tomatoes are one of the few fruits that retain their goodness when cooked and it has been shown that the body absorbs the vitamins more easily when the tomato has been cooked first. So spaghetti sauces and soups are just as good for you as eating raw tomatoes.

Growing tomatoes

Growing tomatoes is normally fairly straightforward even if you don't have green fingers and have never grown any veggies before. Take it step by step and you can't go wrong. Sometimes nature gets in the way, but there are a few tips to get around even the meanest of nature's tricks!

First choose the tomatoes you want to grow. There are so many different varieties, you could be browsing the seed catalogues for hours. Go for a couple of easy types if you've never done this before. Choose a regular everyday garden tomato and maybe a cherry variety.

The larger beefsteak tomatoes take a little longer to mature and can sometimes be difficult to ripen later on in the year. However, if you have a long growing season, or if you just feel a little adventurous, go for it. The smaller tomatoes are wonderful for snacking and mixing into the salad bowl. Choose a yellow plum shape or a tiny red one. The larger varieties are good for making sauces and soups but can still be used in salads and sandwiches.

Once you've decided on your seeds, you need to prepare some growing trays. Fill trays or pots with seed compost and make sure they are well drained. Plants don't like waterlogged soil. Sow seeds according to the instructions on your seed packet. Different varieties will have different growing instructions.

Generally tomato seed should be started off in early spring and kept warm and watered. Keep them warm in a greenhouse or conservatory, or simply on a sunny windowsill. As long as the compost is kept warm and moist, the seeds should germinate within a couple of weeks.

When your plants are a few inches (15–20 cm) tall, re-plant them into individual pots. Make sure the pots are well drained and keep the soil moist. Keep them inside until all danger of frost has passed.

Tomato plant

When the ground has warmed up, normally during May in the UK, put out the pots of tomatoes during the day and bring them in again at night for a few days. This will get them used to outside conditions.

As soon as all danger of frost has passed, plant them out in the garden. They should be about 12 in (30 cm) or more by now. Place a stake firmly in the ground for each plant before planting. Tie the plant gently to the stake and water it well. Allow about 24 in (60 cm) between plants but check on your seed packet for variations.

It's also a good idea to scatter your plants around the garden if you can. If a tomato plant gets blight or any other disease and is growing in a line with other tomato plants, the chances are you will lose the whole line. If they are scattered around the garden you'll give each individual plant more chance of avoiding the viruses.

If the weather gets a little cold, cover the plants in plastic at night to keep them warm. Use a cloche or a similar structure with clear plastic sheets. A cloche is like a miniature polytunnel and can be bought from most garden centres – or you can make one. Find some strong bendy poles, plastic or any other material will do, as long as it has a smooth surface. Push one end of the pole into the ground and bend it over to form an arch. Push the other end in and then repeat this process leaving around 12 in (30 cm) of space between each pole. Make sure the arch is high enough to accommodate your plants. When the line of arches is in place, throw over a sheet of clear plastic and hold it down along each long edge with bricks or logs. The bricks will stop the plastic from flying away, but should be easy enough to move when you need to access your plants. The plastic sheet must be long enough to fold down to the ground at each end to protect the plants from the cold at night.

Keep your tomato plants free from weeds and water them regularly in dry weather. Never let them dry out. During the hot summer months, make sure you water your tomato plants every day, and look for signs of disease. Tomatoes can be fed with an organic fertilizer every couple of weeks during the growing period.

When your plants get a little bigger, they will start producing extra branches between the stem and the main branches. Pinch these out to encourage more fruit rather than foliage. Using your thumb and forefinger squeeze the bottom of the stems of the new branches and twist slightly to remove them from the main plant. A pair of garden scissors will do the job as well, although care should be taken not to damage the main plant.

Note that some people have allergies to tomato plants and gloves should be worn when pinching out the new growth. It's wise to wear gloves anyway to avoid staining your skin.

Once the plants have four or five bunches or 'sets' of fruit/flowers, pinch out the top of the plant to stop it producing any more sets. If the plant keeps producing new sets of fruits, it is unlikely that any will fully develop.

As soon as your tomatoes are fully ripe, pick and eat them! At the end of the season, pull up and compost the plants.

Eating tomatoes

Tomatoes are probably one of the most versatile foods available to us today. And the home grown tomato tastes like no other tomato can taste. Cooked tomatoes hold their vitamin content as well, which is even better!

SALADS

Sliced tomatoes are great mixed into the salad bowl or cut small cherry varieties in half. Chop a large tomato into very small pieces and stir the flesh and seeds of the tomato into a green salad. The tomato will act as a dressing.

Slice medium to large tomatoes on to a serving dish and sprinkle over them a little chopped fennel or basil. Chill for half an hour before serving.

Chop spring onions or shallots and mix with chopped tomatoes. Garnish with a little finely chopped basil. Serve as a side dish.

Cooking with tomatoes

SAUCES

Use fresh tomatoes instead of tinned when making bolognese or chilli sauces. Choose tomatoes that are starting to go soft. Use in lasagne dishes, laying a few slices of a large tomato over the top of the dish when cooked. Grill for a couple of minutes before serving.

OMELETTE

Chop a tomato and mix with beaten eggs and grated cheese to make a tasty summer omelette. Garnish with a couple of slices of tomato and serve with a green salad.

QUICHE

Partly cook a pastry case. Mix beaten eggs, grated cheese, a little grated onion and chopped tomatoes together in a bowl. Pour the mixture into the pastry case and cook for about 30 minutes in a preheated oven at Gas Mark 6, 400°F or 200°C until set. Arrange sliced tomatoes on top of the quiche. Grill under a medium heat for a few minutes to brown off.

STUFFED TOMATOES

Scoop out the inside of large beefsteak tomatoes leaving enough flesh so that the skin remains firm. Stuff with a mixture of cooked meat and vegetables or rice with finely chopped herbs such as fresh basil or coriander. This is a great way to use leftovers. Once filled, place the tomato cases on a baking tray and cook in the centre of a preheated oven, Gas Mark 4, 350°F or 180°C for about 20 minutes. Allow a little longer if you are using meat. When re-heating meat, always make sure it is piping hot right through before serving.

SOUP

Chop an onion and a medium-sized potato and cook in a little butter or oil in a large pan. Don't let it burn. When soft, add as many peeled tomatoes to the pan as possible.

Gently cook the soup until all the tomatoes are soft. Stir regularly. Add a little chopped basil 10 minutes before serving to bring out the tomato taste even more! The soup can be liquidised if you prefer a smooth and creamy texture but it is just as delicious straight out of the pot. Serve with warm crusty bread.

Tip: To make peeling easier, put a few tomatoes at a time in a bowl and carefully pour boiling water over them. Leave for a few minutes and then drain. Rub the skins off as soon as the tomatoes are cool enough to touch.

These are just a few ideas. Tomatoes can be used in so many dishes it's always worth growing a few to show off your culinary skills!

LETTUCE

About lettuce

Lettuce is known to have been cultivated for thousands of years and was considered to represent good luck in China. The milky sap of cos lettuce was used in healing preparations by Roman physicians. Ancient wild varieties of lettuce contained a narcotic similar to opium and leaves were eaten after a meal to encourage sleep. The cultivated lettuce is said to originate from middle Europe.

There are many varieties of modern lettuce, including 'cut-and-come-again' types. These grow like small shrubs, and leaves can be cut from them every day. There are Italian red-tinged curly-leaved lettuces that grow well in a moderate climate, and of course the traditional British-style lettuce with its rich green tender leaves. When choosing your lettuce seed or plants, consider which varieties grow well in your region.

Properties of lettuce

Lettuce is a good source of vitamins A, C and folate, while being low in calories and high in water content. It is an excellent food for the slimmer and interesting enough for any jaded taste buds, or even for the children!

The cos lettuce, also known as *romaine*, tends to be higher in vitamin and mineral content than other varieties. The 'rib' of the cos leaf can be a little bitter in taste, especially in a larger more mature lettuce. Although this part of the cos lettuce has been traditionally used in medicinal preparations, it can be cut out before the rest of the lettuce is added to your meal.

Growing lettuce

There are now many hybrid varieties of lettuce available for growing, and most will thrive in moderate climates. Hot dry weather tends to make lettuce 'bolt'

Lettuce plant

or run to seed, so if you live in a region that enjoys long dry summers, choose a variety that will stand up to those conditions. Butterhead types are resistant to bolting and they come in a number of different varieties.

Get adventurous with lettuce. There are probably hundreds of different varieties you can grow. Try 'cut and come again' types. They grow like small bushes and you can cut from them every day during the height of the season. Also there are the cos type lettuces which are higher in vitamin content than most and will keep fresh for a few days in the fridge. Italian curly-leaved types are wonderful for adding colour and artistic flair to the salad bowl!

Look around in the garden centre local to you and choose varieties that seem to be popular in your area. Chances are they will probably grow well.

Start lettuce off early in the spring and keep seeds warm and watered until the weather is warm enough to put them outside. Fill well-drained seed trays with fresh new compost and sow a few seeds at a time.

Grow different types in each tray and put a marker in so you know what you've planted. When the small plants are large enough to handle they are ready to move. Transplant them carefully into another tray, individual pots or under a cloche outside if the ground is warm enough.

Lettuce seed usually has a high rate of germination and you will probably find you have more plants than you can cope with. The best way to grow lettuce is to plant a few seeds every few weeks throughout the summer months. Plant them directly outside in well prepared soil, after any danger of frost has passed. They are fast growing plants and can be used before they reach maturity if necessary.

Thin out the rows of seedlings and throw the discarded plants into the salad bowl or in a sandwich at lunchtime. Allow space for each plant to grow – check on the seed packets for spacing recommendations. Different types will have different needs. Thin out rows of seedlings when the ground is damp after rain, or water beforehand.

Keep your plants watered and weed free. If the weather gets very dry and sunny, protect with a cover during the hottest part of the day.

Watch out for slugs and snails – lettuce are a feast for the slug family and they can devour a whole line of tender young plants in one evening. Protect the plants with organic slug repellents. Egg shells work well. Crush them and lay round each plant, making sure there are no gaps. The slug will find an entrance if there is one. Sharp sand or gravel can also help. And of course slugs won't go near salt but, as it will dissolve at the slightest hint of damp and then be absorbed by the soil, this isn't an ideal option.

Lettuce plants that are growing outside can also be attacked by birds. If you have a cat, you may not be troubled by birds, otherwise hang a line of old CD discs above the row of lettuce. That will put them off. Birds can get easily tangled up in netting but you can buy very fine mesh netting these days to prevent any injury to wildlife.

Winter lettuce is a good crop to have in the garden. Some varieties may need protection under plastic or glass, but many will put up with very cold nights. Being high in water content though, it's unlikely they will survive a frost.

Grow a couple of plants in a greenhouse or conservatory to have a taste of summer throughout the winter months. Winter crop seeds should be planted in late summer or early autumn. Again check on the advice given on the seed packet. Lettuces can also be grown in pots inside and are a useful indoor plant to grow along with herbs – especially for out-of-season months.

Eating lettuce

The best way to enjoy lettuce and keep it interesting at every meal is to grow as many different varieties as you can. Eating the same lettuce every day can be boring after a while, but with different colours, textures and tastes to choose from, the salad bowl will always be an exciting and tasty meal.

Lettuce is best eaten as fresh as possible and uncooked. Pick a few leaves from each plant in your garden early in the season and make an early spring salad. Remember to use the small lettuces you remove during thinning.

COLOURFUL SALAD
Mix lettuce types together to make a colourful salad bowl. There are lots of different greens and even red variegated lettuces that are easy to grow and delicious to eat.

MIXED SALAD
Finely shred lettuce leaves and mix into the salad bowl with chopped tomatoes, spring onions, peppers and anything else you have available. Stir in a few chopped nuts or sunflower seeds. Serve salad with all summer meals. Omelettes, quiche or chicken off the barbecue all taste better served with a tasty fresh green salad straight from the garden.

LETTUCE ADDITIVE
Chopped lettuce or whole lettuce leaves are a great addition to sandwiches or wraps. Fill a pitta bread with shredded lettuce and add cooked chicken slices or chopped boiled egg, with a little salad dressing or mayonnaise.

Cooking with lettuce
Coarse leaves from lettuces, such as cos, can be mixed with stir fry meals or added to rice or pasta dishes. Slice into thin ribbons and add to dishes during the final couple of minutes of cooking.

SOUP
Chop some spring onions and cook gently in a little oil or melted butter with shredded cos lettuce until the onions are soft. Keep stirring so it doesn't burn. Add some chicken stock and seasoning to taste and cook gently for about 20 minutes. Remove from heat and allow to cool for 10 minutes, then blend in a liquidiser or food processor until smooth. Return to the pan and add about half a cupful of milk and re-heat gently, stirring all the time. Serve piping hot with crusty bread or croutons.

CUCUMBER

About cucumber
There is evidence to suggest that the cucumber has been cultivated in western Asia for around 3,000 years. The Romans were very fond of the cucumber and cultivated it artificially to have it available for consumption all through the year. They were responsible for cucumber spreading across Europe although it took many centuries to reach all corners of Europe and America. By the sixteenth century, the cucumber was established throughout America and Europe.

In the late 1600s, all vegetables that were eaten uncooked were thought to bring on summer diseases and the cucumber therefore took a back seat in the vegetable garden for another couple of hundred years.

The cucumber is a squash and belongs to the same family of plants as pumpkins and gourds. There are many different varieties that can be grown in a mild climate, including some specially cultivated for pickling.

Properties of cucumber

The cucumber is very low in calories and has only a trace of fat making it one of the best diet foods available. One medium-sized cucumber will provide at least 25% of the recommended daily amount of vitamin C. Cucumbers also contain significant amounts of calcium, iron and potassium. They are a natural diuretic and it is also believed that they can help lower blood pressure.

Because they have a high cellulose content, cucumbers can be hard to digest if not chewed properly. People often complain that cucumbers give them indigestion but this can often be corrected with a little more chewing.

Growing cucumber

As the cucumber is originally a tropical plant, in some climates a little extra heat will be needed for the cucumbers to develop to full size. They are often grown in greenhouses or under cloches or cold frames. Where they grow best in your area will depend greatly on the length and temperature of your growing season.

In the UK many gardeners grow cucumbers in greenhouses and cold frames but, in a slightly warmer climate, all varieties can be successfully grown outside. A cold frame is a glass box with a lift-up lid, giving plants protection from cold draughts but still allowing full sun and rain from the top. Cold frames tend to be permanent structures and are a useful addition to the vegetable garden.

When you buy the seed, choose varieties which grow well in your region. The local garden centre should be able to tell you, or ask neighbours and local growers which types they have more success with. As more hybrids become available every year, there will probably be a suitable variety for growing outside in your region.

Start the seed in individual pots in a greenhouse or conservatory. Fill well-drained pots with fresh new compost and sow two seeds in each pot. If possible, buy or make biodegradable pots to start off your cucumber plants. When you transplant them out in the garden, there will be less disturbance to the roots if you can plant the whole pot in the ground.

The cardboard insides from kitchen rolls or toilet rolls are useful for making biodegradable pots for very small plants. Cut them in half across the middle so you have two shorter tubes and put them directly onto a seed tray. Pots can also be made by rolling newspaper or other paper round a rolling pin two or three times, sliding the paper off and folding back one end to make a pot. They only have to stay together a short while and, if you fill a seed tray with pots, they hold each other up very well, especially when they are full of compost. Otherwise, pot-making kits are readily available in garden centres.

If making your own pots isn't possible, you can still successfully re-plant the small plants but be careful not to handle them too much. Make sure the compost is damp before removing from the pot and ease the plant out gently, handling it as little as possible.

Plant out when the weather warms up and all danger of frost has passed. Allow a fairly large space for the plants to grow into. Check on your seed packet for growing recommendations, but they will normally need about 2–3 ft (60–90 cm) per plant all round.

Cucumber plant

Some growers use a ridge method where the plants are grown on a small hill of earth. Your seed packet may suggest this as the best way for your variety. Always check the growing recommendations before you start.

Keep an eye out for slugs while your plants are small. Protect them with organic slug repellents. Crushed egg shells spread around plants deter slugs, and they withstand a little rain too. Or try an old country method: slugs are attracted to beer and will drown in a bowl of beer rather than attack your baby plants – with a little luck. You will have to dispose of a bowl of dead drunk slugs in the morning though!

Keep the plants weed-free and watered. Pull weeds by hand rather than using a hoe. Young plants can be easily damaged by large tools. Cucumber plants trail over a fairly large area and, once grown, few weeds can battle through the undergrowth. Frogs and toads love the semi-tropical cover of cucumbers and other squash plants, and they will also keep slugs and snails to a minimum. Encourage frogs to your garden if you can.

Some varieties of cucumber will require male flowers to be removed, or the fruits will be bitter in taste or won't develop at all. There are so many hybrid types available now that you will probably find one that doesn't need too much attention.

When the cucumber fruits start to grow, make sure they are not trailing on wet soil. Lift them gently onto a dry patch or lay straw underneath each one.

When the cucumber fruit can easily be twisted away from the stalk, it's ready to eat. With good conditions and a long warm summer, cucumbers can be very prolific. Be prepared to give some away!

Eating cucumber

Cucumber is generally eaten raw and fresh in salads and makes excellent sauces and dips to serve with hot dishes.

CUCUMBER DIP

Remove some, or all, of the peel from a cucumber. Chop the remaining flesh into fairly small pieces. The seeds can be discarded or left in according to taste and time available. Stir into a sauce made of half mayonnaise and half natural yoghurt, or a low fat *crème fraiche* mix.

CHILLED SUMMER SOUP

Peel a couple of cucumbers, chop and mix them with the flesh of an avocado and some chopped mint leaves. Blend in a food processor until liquidised. Chill before serving.

SNACKS

Cucumber is a tasty aid to losing weight and makes an excellent snack. Cut into sticks and mix with carrot sticks and green or red pepper. Cucumber sticks are great for kids' lunchboxes and children love the fresh, slightly sweet taste.

SANDWICHES

For a healthy low calorie sandwich, spread cottage cheese, or any very low fat cheese, onto a slice of rye bread or low calorie crispbread. Finely slice a cucumber and pile it onto the cheese. Don't scrimp on the cucumber slices. The more you eat, the better for you.

Cucumber sandwiches have long been a favourite at elegant tea parties. Tiny triangle sandwiches without the crusts have been considered a food fit for royalty for many generations.

PICKLED CUCUMBER

There are a number of ways of pickling cucumber. A traditional method is to lay slices of peeled cucumber in a bowl and layer with salt. Leave it for 24 hours, then rinse and allow to dry a little. Put the salted cucumber into a jar with pickling vinegar. Seal the jar and leave it for about a month before using.

Another way is to score down the cucumber then cut into slices. Sprinkle about a teaspoon or two of salt over the slices and leave for about ten minutes, then rinse. Put the cucumber into a jar with white wine vinegar and, if liked, a little bruised ginger, and leave overnight. This recipe can be eaten the following day. Any leftover pickle can be refrigerated but will only remain fresh for a few days.

PEPPERS

About peppers

Peppers have been grown for thousands of years but they became more of an everyday food around the sixteenth century, especially in India and Europe.

There are many different types of pepper, but the two main species are chilli peppers and sweet peppers. It's fun to grow a few chilli pepper plants for those extra spicy dishes but sweet peppers are more versatile and are still relatively easy to grow. Sweet peppers are known as 'bell peppers' in many places. They can be used raw in salads and as a cooked vegetable.

Generally, sweet peppers are red, yellow or green. It can be difficult in a short growing season to produce healthy red or yellow peppers although, with a little greenhouse help, it's possible. Green peppers are easily cultivated and will produce many fruits in the ideal conditions.

Properties of peppers

Peppers have a high vitamin content and are an excellent food for those convalescing after an illness. Mature red peppers have twice as much vitamin C as green peppers, so if you can grow a few it's worthwhile. Peppers aid a weight loss diet in as much as they are very low calorie and high vitamin foods. They help the body absorb calcium and iron, making them a good digestive aid as well. Weight for weight, peppers have a higher content of vitamins A and C than many other fruit and vegetables.

Chilli peppers are sometimes very hot, and should be eaten in moderation or not at all, depending on the delicacy of your stomach! Research indicates that hot spicy foods can increase the metabolism so they could be a welcome addition to a well-balanced diet.

Growing peppers

Sweet pepper seed can be started in late spring. It's very tempting to start them off early when there is a break in the weather, but peppers often become stunted and don't produce such a good harvest if they are started too early.

Prepare well-drained seed trays with fresh new compost and sow according to the recommendations on your seed packet. Generally, this will be in March or April. Keep the soil damp but never waterlogged. Peppers are a high water content plant and will rot quickly in very wet soil, but they shouldn't be allowed to dry out completely.

When your plants are large enough to handle, or when they have three or four true leaves, they can be transplanted into pots of fresh compost to grow on before they're put outside. Let them grow for another couple of weeks or so, keeping pots damp and warm. Don't put them outside before all danger of a frost has passed. Mid May is usually a safe time in the UK.

Choose a sunny spot, but not in the same soil that had potatoes or tomatoes growing during the previous year. Peppers belong to the same plant family and can pick up leftover bugs or viruses from the soil where tomato or potato plants have grown over the previous couple of years. If you are growing both sweet and chilli peppers, keep them as wide apart in the garden as possible to avoid cross-pollination.

Your plants will need about 12–18 in (30–45 cm) of all round space to grow, and should be gently transplanted, handling as little as possible. Protect them from slugs in the early stages of development. Slugs eat through the stem and can kill a whole line of peppers in one sitting.

Keep weeds away and water regularly, especially in hot dry weather. Although peppers enjoy a sunny spot in the garden, sometimes the midday sun can scorch the plants and dry them out too quickly. Watch out for this and be ready to protect the plants with some shade if necessary. Special sheets can be found at good garden centres that will protect your plants from the sun. Remember to remove the sheet though to allow the peppers to breathe.

Pepper plants are often available in markets and garden centres in early spring. These plants were brought on inside or artificially, so they have to be acclimatised before putting out into the garden. Keep them indoors or in the greenhouse for a few weeks. They won't be frost hardy and probably won't survive a cold night.

Pepper plant

Peppers can be grown indoors as house plants, although they should be placed in a very light place. If they are placed on a windowsill, make sure direct sunlight doesn't burn the leaves. They will need watering regularly, but never let pots become waterlogged.

Peppers can also be grown in well-drained pots and containers on a patio or around the garden. Move the pots out of direct sunlight if they start drying out. Remember to move them back into sun again though or the fruits won't develop. Pots and containers dry out quickly, so water regularly.

If you are growing peppers in a greenhouse, polytunnel or under a cloche, they should be aired regularly. Gently loosen the soil around the stems to avoid fungus or mould building up. Use a very small hand tool to avoid damaging the plants.

A healthy patch of pepper plants resembles a mini-rainforest and is an attractive feature in a vegetable garden. The plants will grow on quite late in the year, and can be protected from cold nights with a cloche.

As soon as the peppers can be twisted from the plant easily, they are ripe and ready to eat.

Eating peppers

Peppers are a versatile kitchen food and can be cooked as a vegetable or eaten raw. Green peppers tend to be crisper although the skin can be a little tougher than red or yellow peppers.

SNACKS

Peppers can be cut into strips and served with carrot and cucumber sticks as healthy snacks. Serve with a low fat garlic dip or a simple mayonnaise and plain yoghurt sauce.

SALADS

Thinly slice peppers into sticks or small cubes and mix into a chopped green salad. Cut into larger chunks to mix into a chunkier salad. Use a selection of colours if you have them available. Red and yellow peppers brighten up a green salad. Slice peppers into rings and lay on the top of the salad bowl as an edible garnish.

Cooking with peppers

Peppers can be cooked as a vegetable and can be added to many dishes to add bulk as well as nutrition.

STIR-FRIES

Cut peppers into fine strips and add to the pan a few minutes before serving to keep crisp, or add earlier during cooking if you prefer your peppers a little softer.

CHILLIES AND ONE-POT MEALS

Peppers can be added to many dishes including bolognese, chilli recipes and even traditional shepherd's pies and meat pies. They are also a good vegetable to add bulk to a vegetarian dish. Chop peppers and either simmer in a little boiling water for a few minutes before adding to the rest of the ingredients, or fry gently in a little oil.

STUFFED PEPPERS

Cut the top off peppers with a sharp knife and put to one side. Remove the seeds. Cook some rice and mix with very finely chopped tomato and a little cooked onion. A clove or two of chopped or crushed garlic and some herbs can be added according to taste. Cooked mince can also be used, but care should be taken that re-heated meat is piping hot right through before serving.

Carefully spoon the mixture into the pepper cases and put the tops back on. Cook in a medium oven for about half an hour or until the pepper is tender and the stuffing is hot right through. When cooked, take the top off and sprinkle a little grated cheese on top. Grill under a medium heat until the cheese melts. Serve hot with a salad.

ONIONS

About onions

Onions have, literally, been around just about forever. They have been cultivated for about 5,000 years and records indicate that they grew wild and were eaten in prehistoric times. There are many different types of onions you can grow, from tree onions to everyday ones. The choice is yours. If you have enough space, grow a few different varieties and have onions all year round.

The ancient Egyptians believed onions to have magical powers and they have been used for medicinal purposes for thousands of years. A common remedy for a dry cough is still used today and is very effective.

Properties of onions

Onions are one of the few vegetables that have been proved to help balance insulin levels. They can significantly help reduce cholesterol and the risk of heart disease. They are also a good source of vitamin C and B vitamins.

As well as being high in dietary fibre they are low in calories and another very versatile and tasty vegetable. Onions are a wholesome addition to a diet and can help ward off colds and flu symptoms as well as being a very effective medicine for coughs. Chop an onion and leave overnight in a bowl with a cover. The following morning, the juice from the onion should be sipped slowly to alleviate cough symptoms.

Growing onions

Because of the vast range of onions you can grow, it would be impossible to cover them all here. There are many 'specialist' onions that originate from other than mild climates and these will need particular care. There should be manufacturer's growing recommendations with the seeds or 'sets' when you buy them.

To grow a regular crop of everyday kitchen onions, it's best to buy the seed in the form of bulbs or 'sets'. Garden centres stock these during the winter and early spring. It's possible to grow everyday onions from seed, but they do need extra care in the early stages and germination can take some time as well as being rather hit and miss.

Dig over the ground as soon as it is workable in the spring and rake finely, removing any weeds and large stones. Plant the onion sets allowing about 6–8 in (15–20 cm) of growing room. Leave about 18 in between rows.

Pull out weeds as they appear and water regularly. The ground must be well drained. Onion sets will rot if left in waterlogged soil.

Onion growing

In hot dry weather onions sometimes run to seed or 'bolt'. If this happens, you will notice a woody stem growing straight up between the leaves. Break this off or bend it down if possible and let the plant grow on a little longer. Pick and use these onions. Onions that have run to seed have a hollow centre and will not store well.

When the onion leaves are dying back, bend over to the ground and leave for as long as the weather holds. On a sunny morning, pull the onions and lay on the dry soil for a day in the sun to dry out. Turn a few times during the day and keep them apart to allow air to circulate.

After your onions have dried out in the sun, plait them in strings or lay in dry wooden or cardboard boxes. Keep in a dry place out of direct light and they will keep for many months.

SPRING ONIONS

Spring onions should be started early in the spring in seedbeds or trays of fresh new compost. Sow seed *in situ*, preferably in a seedbed finely worked and clear of weeds and large stones. Check on your seed packet as some varieties germinate better by scattering the seed and raking it in gently rather than covering it.

When the onions are crowding in on each other, carefully thin out. Make sure the ground is wet before thinning and gently lift out the weaker plants where possible, leaving a couple of inches of growing room for each onion. Use in the summer as required.

EVERLASTING ONIONS
Sometimes known as Welsh onions, everlasting onions literally will last forever. They do need a certain amount of attention. The best way to start your everlasting patch is to begin with a clump of onions either bought or donated from another grower in spring or autumn.

Separate the onions carefully, leaving as much root intact as possible and plant out in the spring or autumn, allowing about 2 ft (60 cm) of growing room for each plant. They look rather lonely with all this space when you first plant them out but, after a few months, they will be filling the gaps. Each bulb multiplies and will produce anything from 6 to 12 new onions.

Autumn plantings will be ready in the spring and come at a moment when there is little else available in the garden. Dig up a whole clump, use what you need in the kitchen and plant out a couple of strong rooted bulbs for autumn picking. Repeat with all the clumps. You can increase your patch by simply planting out more than you started with.

Use the everlasting onions or dig up and re-plant. If left too long, the plants will keep growing but the centre will begin to die back.

Eating onions

No chef would be without onions, and a string of home grown organic onions hanging in the corner will inspire anyone to get imaginative in the kitchen. If you suffer with watering eyes when you are chopping onions, and the stronger the onion the worse it is, try cutting from the top of the onion and leaving the root end until last. Running water slowly over the onion helps, although this isn't easy to do while you are cutting them.

RAW ONIONS
Raw onions can be very strong in taste and aren't always palatable. Spring onions, everlasting onions and other varieties of hybrid special onions are often milder and can be added to salads and eaten alone.

ONION AND TOMATO SALAD
Slice onions and tomatoes and sprinkle mixed herbs or chopped basil over the top. Chill for about 30 minutes before serving. Use shallots or milder onions if preferred.

PICKLED ONIONS
Pickling onions are slightly different to the regular kitchen onion, but they can be grown in the vegetable garden. Peel onions and put into sterilised jars. Pour pickling spiced vinegar over them to cover and seal the jars. Leave for a month or two before using.

GARNISH
Chopped spring onions, or ordinary onions if liked, can be used as a garnish on many meals as well as salad. Top cheese on toast with finely sliced spring onions or sprinkle on a cottage pie or omelette.

Cooking with onions
There aren't many dishes you can't add onions to, and the blandest meal will come alive with a little chopped onion added during cooking.

ONE-POT MEALS
Add chopped onions to the recipe early in the cooking time as they take a while to soften. Onions can be added to bolognese, chilli dishes, cottage pies

and any other combination of mince-type meals you can produce. Onions bring out the flavour of mince.

Onions are also a wonderful addition to stews and casseroles, in slices or whole if they are small enough.

STIR-FRIES
Finely chopped or sliced onions can be added to almost any stir-fry meal, although they should be used in moderation as the onion will be less cooked and therefore stronger in taste.

BAKED ONION
Large onions can be baked and stuffed for an extra special addition to a Sunday roast. Peel the onion and carefully cut off about an inch from the top. Scoop out some of the inside and fill with cheese and a little chopped cooked bacon or vegetarian substitute. Bake in a medium oven until the onion is soft and the stuffing is piping hot right through.

ONION SOUP
Gently cook chopped onions in a little butter or oil in a heavy-based saucepan. Stir to prevent burning. Cook until the onions are golden brown and stir in a couple of tablespoons of flour. Mix well and add chicken or vegetable stock slowly, stirring to prevent lumps forming from the flour. If you have trouble with this stage, you can make a paste of flour and stock and then add this to the pan.

Add seasoning to taste and bring slowly to the boil, stirring regularly. Reduce heat and simmer for about 20 minutes. Serve with hot crusty bread or small triangles of cheese on toast.

CHAPTER 2

DOWN TO ROOTS

Root vegetables haven't always had a good image, probably because they are often covered in dirt and can be fairly dull in colour. But lurking beneath the somewhat unattractive exterior lies a world of nutrition waiting to be discovered.

This chapter covers five wholesome and nutritious root vegetables, all of which can be eaten as a separate vegetable or added to stews, casseroles and pickles and wines:

- carrots

- beetroot

- parsnips

- salsify

- potatoes.

Nearly all root vegetables can be added to stews, casseroles and curries. Most can be roasted and steamed and some can even be sautéed. Although salsify isn't a commonly found supermarket vegetable, it has been traditionally part of the kitchen garden for many years and is relatively easy to grow taking up little space and time.

Potatoes aren't truly a root vegetable but, as they live beneath the ground, we'll consider them roots for the moment. They are, botanically speaking, a tuber – a swelling from the root of the plant. Potatoes are a staple food and are probably one of the most wholesome vegetables we can grow in the garden. They are also practical and can be served hundreds of different ways!

Many root vegetables can be stored successfully for weeks, if not months, in a dry place out of light. Don't wash before storing. Dry and brush off excess soil then either place them in single layers in a cardboard or wooden box, in a barrel of sand or store in cloth sacks. Excess root vegetables can be pickled or made into wine.

There are some tasty recipes included for each root vegetable in this chapter proving they really are worth their weight in gold.

CARROTS

About carrots

We tend to think of carrots as long and slim, bright orange in colour and something you must eat if you want to see in the dark. Carrots are so much more than that though. There are many different varieties that will grow readily in the home garden, some with short fat roots, others long and slender. There are also other colours available.

Carrots have been cultivated for thousands of years and records indicate that different coloured carrots were grown, from black and purple through to reds and yellows. In Holland, in the mid sixteenth century, red and yellow carrots were crossed to create the orange variety we know so well today.

As well as being a wholesome and nutritious root vegetable, carrots have been used in medicinal preparations throughout the centuries. The Ancient Greeks believed them to be an effective aphrodisiac.

Properties of carrots

Carrots are reputed to help us see in the dark. This is probably due to the natural beta-carotene, a form of vitamin A. They also contain vitamins B1 and B6 and significant quantities of calcium and iron.

Carrots can be eaten raw or cooked and, because of their sweet flavour, are a vegetable that can be used in dishes such as carrot cake, as well as nourishing stews, casseroles and soups. Young children like the sweet taste of carrots and they should be encouraged to enjoy them. Get your children out into the garden with you and let them grow their own.

Growing carrots

Carrots, like all root vegetables, prefer a good depth of soil to develop fully. However, there are new varieties on the market that are shorter and fatter and these types should be chosen if you have shallow top soil in your garden.

Dig the soil over in the spring to a depth of about 12 in (30 cm) and remove large stones, non-organic debris and any perennial weeds. Mix in some well-rotted fertiliser or compost if the soil is a little tired. If possible, fertiliser should be incorporated into the soil during the previous autumn. Make sure whatever you dig in is well rotted though, or the carrots will fork, or split, and won't develop properly.

Check on your seed packet for growing recommendations, but generally carrot seed is started mid to late spring. Rake over your seed bed or vegetable patch to a fine tilth and sow very short lines of seed every couple of weeks or so right through until late summer if the weather is good enough. 'Tilth' is a word used for the cultivated soil prepared for crops. So a 'fine tilth' is crumbly soil like breadcrumbs, although not as fine!

There is a good reason for sowing short lines of carrot seed. When the plants are about 2–3 in tall (5 cm or more) they will need thinning and with a long line of carrot plants this can be a daunting chore.

Carrots tend to be slow to germinate and you need to keep an eye on the area while you are waiting for them to start growing. Make sure the ground doesn't dry out or become waterlogged (carrot seed won't germinate at all in waterlogged ground). And keep weeds away. Carrot foliage is feathery, right from the start, so anything that doesn't look like a carrot plant should be pulled out. Pull weeds gently so as not to disturb the carrot seeds, and always by hand. A tool at this stage will damage the seeds.

When your carrots are ready to thin, choose a damp day and make sure the soil is fairly wet before you start. The plants will pull out more easily and you won't disturb the ones you leave. Thin carrots by removing the weaker ones

Carrot plants

32

where possible and leave an inch between the plants for growth. After a couple of weeks, this whole process will need repeating and then again, until each carrot has around 4 in (10 cm) to grow into. Double check on your seed packet as fatter varieties may need more space.

On the second and third thinning, you will be pulling up tiny carrots. These can be eaten and are perfect for mixing into a salad bowl or adding bulk to a casserole or stew.

When your carrots are thinned, let them grow on until they are full size and pull them as you need them. Keep them watered in dry weather, and don't let them get bogged down with weeds.

Remember to plant a short line every couple of weeks or so to keep a constant supply going. Short lines of carrots can be planted in the herb bed or amongst the flowers if you are stretched for space. As long as they are not too shaded and get enough water they will grow just as well as if they were in the vegetable patch. If your plants don't grow well, it could be because the soil is depleted of minerals and needs feeding. Use an organic fertiliser to boost the productivity, but not fresh manure.

Eating carrots

Carrots are a wonderfully adaptable vegetable in the kitchen. They can be eaten raw or cooked and can be added to sweet dishes as well as main meals.

SNACKS

Carrot sticks are a great way of adding colour and sweetness to, sometimes boring, 'healthy foods' especially where kids are concerned. Very young children shouldn't be given raw carrot as it takes a lot of chewing and there is a danger of choking. For older children, however, carrot sticks make a great packed lunch addition.

SALADS

Carrots can be added to just about any type of salad. They add colour and plenty of vitamins to the meal. The most difficult choice is how to cut them. Carrots can be sliced into rings; make them as thin as possible when adding to a salad bowl. They can be carefully cut into matchstick shapes or grated. Whatever the shape you decide on, carrots can be mixed into any green salad. Grated carrots also make an attractive garnish.

Cooking with carrots

Carrots can be steamed or boiled, stir-fried and even roasted. And of course they can be used to make the infamous carrot cake.

CARROT CAKE

Because carrot cake has never been among the 'cheap' cakes in the shop, we tend to think it must be complicated to make. It isn't!

Scrub four medium-sized carrots and grate them finely. Peel the carrots if they haven't been grown organically. Put the grated carrots in a mixing bowl with about 8 oz (200 g) of self-raising flour or plain flour with a couple of teaspoons of baking powder. Add 5 oz (120 g) of sugar, a handful of raisins, two mashed bananas, two beaten eggs and 5 fl oz of light cooking oil. Sprinkle over a teaspoon or two of mixed spice or cinnamon. If you have a couple of ounces of broken walnut pieces, add them as well. Blend all the ingredients together and bake in a lightly greased cake tin for about an hour in the centre of a moderate oven: Gas Mark 4, 350°F or 180°C. Cool and cover with a topping or eat warm as it is.

The traditional topping for carrot cake is a blend of cream cheese and icing sugar. Start with about 7 oz (50 g) of cream cheese in a bowl and blend with 2 oz (50 g) of unsalted butter. Add 2 oz (50 g) of icing sugar and blend until it reaches the required consistency. If you like a drier topping add more icing sugar. A teaspoon of flavouring, such as vanilla, can be added if preferred. Spread evenly over the cake when it is completely cold.

BOILED BEEF AND CARROTS

This is a well-established old English recipe. Carrots and beef are a perfect combination of tastes. Always add a few carrot slices to beef casseroles and stews. Whole baby carrots can be used and have the sweetest flavour. Allow a little extra cooking time for whole carrots.

STIR-FRIES

Cut carrots into very fine sticks before adding to the pan. Cook for just a few minutes so that they keep their crunch.

ONE-POT MEALS

As well as stews and casseroles, carrots can be mixed into bolognese, chilli dishes and lasagne. Chop carrots into small pieces before adding to your recipe.

BEETROOT

About beetroot

Beetroot is believed to have originated from a sea plant that grew extensively over Europe and Asiatic coastlines. The root had been used in medicinal preparations for many centuries but not in the kitchen until around the seventeenth century. The leaves of beetroot were used as a green vegetable and the roots were slow to develop into the globe shape we know today.

Beetroot leaves can be used like spinach, although removing too many leaves can stunt the root growth. Grow a few for the leaves and let the others develop into a healthy root.

The roots of beetroot were used in ancient times to treat many ailments, including fevers and constipation.

Properties of beetroot

Beetroot is packed with vitamins and minerals and has a high natural sugar content, making it an extremely useful food to include in a healthy well-balanced diet.

Beetroot is a good source of folate, vitamin C and dietary fibre, and the rich red pigment has been proven to fight against free radicals in the body. Beetroot is said to prolong life and probably does with all the minerals and vitamins it contains.

It can be stored easily and is a good root vegetable to grow for pickling and using in the winter months.

Growing beetroot

Before you buy beetroot seed, check you have the right variety. Some beetroot is grown specifically for the leafy tops and others for the swollen globe-shaped root. The seeds bred for leafy growth probably won't produce fully mature roots.

Choose a fairly sunny position in the garden and dig over the ground to a depth of about 12 in (30 cm) or more. Beetroot will tolerate part shade but will need some sun and a light airy spot to thrive. The ground should be well drained with no chance of becoming waterlogged. Remove any large stones, non-organic debris and perennial weeds. Dig in some well-rotted manure in the season before planting, if necessary, and a little lime if your soil is very acidic. Don't add fresh manure or very rich compost just before planting, as this will cause the roots to fork.

Rake the ground over to a fine tilth and sow seed in late spring very sparsely along a row. Beetroot seeds are normally 'multiple' and will need thinning later on. One seed should be sown every couple of inches. They are fairly large and

Beetroot plant

easy to handle although it's always best to handle seeds as gently and as little as possible.

Once you have sown the seed, water well and keep free of weeds. When the seeds germinate they will produce small clumps of plants and the weaker ones should be removed. Wait until the ground is wet or water first before thinning plants. Gently remove the weaker plants leaving one every couple of inches to grow on. Firm the soil down around the plants you leave in the ground.

After two or three weeks it may be necessary to thin the plants again, eventually leaving around 6 in (15 cm) of space per plant. Double check on your seed packet as varieties differ. Larger beetroot types will need a larger space to grow into.

Watch out for birds when your plants are small. The red leaves are very attractive to birds and the plants may need netting until they become established. Use a bird-friendly net if needed.

Keep watered and free from weeds and loosen the soil gently around the stem of the plants from time to time. Use a small hand tool for this rather than a hoe. Beetroots grow close to the surface of the soil and a hoe could easily damage them.

Unless you have chosen a particularly large hybrid variety, beetroot should be harvested when they are about 3 in (7 or 8 cm) in diameter or they can become woody and lose their taste.

If you have a good crop, it's worth using a few when they are small. Tender young roots are nutritious and delicious and always worth a treat or two.

Harvest all beetroot before the first frost of winter. Twist off the tops rather than cutting them. This prevents the red pigment from 'bleeding'. Dry the roots but do not wash before storing. Beetroot can be stored for several days, and sometimes weeks, in a dark airy place. Beetroot is traditionally pickled for storing.

Eating beetroot

Although beetroot is traditionally cooked and pickled, there are many other ways of serving this very wholesome and nutritious vegetable.

SALADS

Raw beetroot can be grated and added to salads. Peel first and grate finely. Stir into any mixed salad or use as a garnish for green salads or hard-boiled eggs.

BEETROOT AND POTATO SALAD

Cook beetroots in boiling water until tender. Drain and set aside to cool. Peel and cut potatoes into chunks and steam or boil. Drain and leave to cool. When potatoes and beetroots are completely cold, cut them into small cubes and mix together in a bowl with a finely chopped onion.

Stir a chopped pepper into some natural yoghurt and mix carefully with the vegetables. Garnish with a little parsley or chopped chives.

PICKLED BEETROOT

Small beetroots are best for pickling mainly because they are easy to fit in jars. Find large sealable jars and wash before use. Place on their sides in a slow oven until dry.

Twist off the leaves of your beetroots and rinse. Place in a large pan and cover with water. Bring to the boil, then reduce heat and simmer until the beetroots are cooked. To check that they are cooked, carefully rub your thumb against the skin. If it starts to peel away easily, they should be ready. Drain and cool completely. Put into jars and pour over pickling vinegar. Seal the jars and label. Store in a cool place out of direct light.

Cooking with beetroot

Simmer beetroot with skins on until tender. Drain and cool. Remove the peel and cut into thin slices or dice. Serve with any dish as a cold vegetable, or eat while still warm. Cold, cooked beetroot is particularly good with salads, as well as boiled eggs.

BEETROOT SOUP

Chop an onion, one or two cloves of garlic and two stalks of celery. Place in a large pan with a little water and light cooking oil. Cook until soft, stirring to prevent sticking or burning.

Peel and grate a parsnip, one or two carrots and six small beetroot. Add to the pan with 2.5 pt (1.25 l) of chicken or vegetable stock, and bring to the boil. Reduce heat and simmer for 30 to 40 minutes until vegetables are tender. Serve hot with crusty bread.

PARSNIPS

About parsnips

Parsnips have been around for thousands of years and would grow wild over most of Europe if left to their own devices. They have always been a hardy root crop and were popular in Roman times as an everyday vegetable. They have been an important root crop for many years.

Because of their sweet flavour, parsnips have been used in sweet dishes as well as savoury. In medieval times they were added to bread recipes and also given to babies to soothe digestion. They are often still used to make wine and beer in rural areas.

Parsnips will re-seed themselves in a home garden and can become intrusive if not checked. They are easy to grow and will survive a mild winter. Parsnips taste even better after the first frost.

Properties of parsnips

Parsnips are closely related to the carrot, and very old recipes could have mistaken the two. They are higher in minerals and vitamin content than carrots, particularly in vitamin B5 (pantothenic acid). They are also a good source of dietary fibre and are rich in potassium. All in all, they are a very wholesome root vegetable.

After the first frost of the year, they contain more natural sugar and are sweeter to taste.

Care should be taken if collecting wild parsnips as the plant is very similar to hemlock, which is poisonous.

Growing parsnips

To start your parsnips, it's best to buy seeds from a good supplier as germination can be erratic from seed collected from your own plants.

There are a number of different varieties of parsnip available. Some are short and some produce longer roots. If you have very shallow fertile soil, choose a shorter type.

As with all root crops, parsnips will fork if planted in manure-rich soil. If the soil needs a boost, well-rotted compost or manure should be dug into the ground during the previous autumn.

Parsnips like a sunny position and should be positioned carefully in the garden as they are a long growing crop and will occupy space in the vegetable bed for a large part of the year.

Dig over the ground as deeply as you can and remove any large stones and perennial weeds. Rake over and sow seed directly outside. Parsnips won't transplant well so they should be sown *in situ*. Sow fairly thickly and handle the seed as little as possible. They should be sown in the spring, but check on

Parsnip plants

the growing recommendations for your particular variety before sowing. Leave about 18–24 in (45–61 cm) between rows.

When the plants are a couple of inches (5 cm) high, thin them by pulling out the weaker ones and leaving one plant every inch or so to grow on. Do this when the ground is wet or water it first. Gently firm down the soil around the plants you leave.

Thin again in a couple of weeks to allow about 4 in (10 cm) between plants. Fatter varieties may need slightly more space. Double-check the instructions on your seed packet. The small parsnips you pull out can be added to soups and stews to add bulk and loads of goodness.

Keep watered and weed free. Hoe gently from time to time, or loosen the ground with a hand trowel or fork to avoid damaging the roots.

As soon as the roots have developed, they can be eaten, probably not before late summer or early autumn though. Parsnips are known to taste better after the first frost of the year and many growers wait until then before eating them.

Parsnips can be stored for a few weeks in a cloth sack or laid in single layers in a cardboard or wooden box. Keep out of direct light and store in a dry, airy environment.

Leave a few plants in the ground to flower and produce seed for next year's planting. When the flower head starts to dry, place a cloth around the plants to collect the seed as it falls. Keep the seeds in a dry place until next spring. Otherwise, you can leave the seeds to fall and germinate where they land. They may not survive a very cold winter though. Collect a few and leave a few, but remember you will need to sow more seed from your own plants than you would if using bought seed.

Cooking with parsnips

Parsnips are a lot more versatile than they first appear. There are a number of ways to eat them and all are worth trying.

STEAMED

Scrub or peel non-organically grown parsnips and rinse. Cut into slices and steam or boil for about 10 minutes or until tender. Drain and return to the pan. Add a knob of butter and some chopped fresh or dried herbs. Stir gently and serve hot.

ROASTED

Scrub or peel parsnips and cut them into large chunks or through the middle from top to tail. Either roast them around a joint of meat, or in their own pan with a little oil and mixed herbs if liked. Cook in a medium to hot oven for about 40 minutes or until cooked through. Turn over halfway through cooking. Parsnips can be dry roasted on a non-stick pan. Par boil for 5 minutes and drain well before laying them on the cooking tray.

PARSNIP SOUP

This recipe includes coriander, giving a mild curry flavour but it can be left out if preferred. You will need about 2 lbs (900 g) of parsnips, peeled or scrubbed and cut into small pieces, as well as one or two onions also peeled and chopped. Gently heat about 2 oz (50 g) of butter in a large pan and cook onions and parsnips for a few minutes. Stir to prevent burning.

Stir in a couple of tablespoons of flour, or make a paste of flour (or cornflour) and a little water before adding to the pan. It needs to be smooth to avoid lumps of flour in the soup.

Slowly add about 2.5 pt (1.5 l) of vegetable or chicken stock and stir in a handful of chopped fresh coriander. Bring to the boil, reduce heat and simmer for 45 to 50 minutes or until the vegetables are tender.

Remove from the heat and cool for 10 minutes. Blend in a liquidiser or food processor until smooth, then return to the pan. Heat through on a very low heat for a few minutes, stirring all the time. Serve hot, sprinkled with a garnish of very finely chopped coriander.

PARSNIP SALAD
Very young parsnips can be lightly boiled or steamed, drained well and left to cool before adding to any salad.

PARSNIP SNACKS
Scrub or peel, and finely slice parsnips. Slice them with a peeler if possible to make them extra fine. Deep-fry the slices in hot oil for about three minutes. Drain on kitchen paper and then re-fry for another minute. Drain again and sprinkle with a little sea salt before serving.

SALSIFY

About salsify
Salsify isn't a vegetable we hear of much these days, and it is rarely available in supermarkets or grocers. Occasionally it can be found in local markets from late autumn through the winter months, but to be sure of a good supply of this wonderful hardy root crop, it's a good idea to grow it yourself.

Salsify is sometimes called 'oyster plant' as, when cooked, it has a slight taste of oysters. The root is similar to a long thin parsnip and can grow to 12 in or more. Salsify needs a good depth of soil to fully develop.

The plant produces an attractive flower and can be grown in borders and left in the ground right through the winter months.

Salsify has grown wild for thousands of years across Europe and up until the sixteenth century it was considered to be helpful in treating snakebites as well as diseases such as the plague. It wasn't cultivated until the Middle Ages and since then it has gone in and out of fashion in the kitchen garden.

Properties of salsify

Salsify contains many of the B vitamins as well as vitamins A and C. It also contains significant amounts of calcium, potassium and dietary fibre. It has no cholesterol or fat and is a nutritious winter vegetable. After the first frost the natural sugar increases in the root and salsify is said to be very good for diabetics because of the high levels of fructose.

The young leaves of the plant can be eaten in salads, although it's best not to strip too many leaves as you want the plant to put its energy into developing a strong healthy root.

Growing salsify

Scorzonera is often grown in place of salsify. It is a similar crop in the same family of plants but has a stronger taste. It is also perennial so will re-seed itself and produce a permanent patch in the garden. Salsify, however, is an annual plant and will need to be planted every year.

The most important factor in growing salsify successfully is the depth of soil. Because of its hardiness it will probably grow just about anywhere in the garden. Try growing a short line in full sun and another in partial shade and compare the two. Salsify stays in the ground for a long time, right up until late autumn and in some cases can be left in the ground right through the winter months, making it a very useful winter crop for the kitchen garden.

Although the roots need depth of soil to fully develop, the plants don't take up much room in the vegetable bed and can be used as border plants to save space, or grown amongst the herbs or flowerbeds.

Salsify plants

As soon as the ground is workable in early spring or late winter, dig over to a depth of 18 inches or more if possible. Remove any perennial weeds and large stones from the area and rake to a fine tilth. Salsify seed can be sown early in the year and will benefit from a frost or two in the early stages of its development.

Make a trench half an inch to an inch deep (1 or 2 cm). Sow seed thinly along the line and cover with fine soil. Check on your seed packet for variations before you start. Leave around 12 in (30 cm) between rows.

When the seeds have germinated and seedlings are a couple of inches high, they may need thinning depending on how thickly you sowed the seed. Do this when the ground is wet. Water first if necessary. Pull out the weaker plants leaving about 8–12 in (20–30 cm) of growing room per plant. (Again, double-check on your seed packet for any variations.)

Water and keep the plants weed free. Salsify is a hardy plant and needs very little looking after once established. The plants are long growing and will stay in the ground right through until the following winter, and rarely suffer from diseases or pest attacks. Use as soon as the roots have developed, generally from the beginning of autumn.

When digging up, loosen the soil around the plant with a fork, being careful not to damage the roots. You will need to dig deep if the soil has become compact. Don't pull the plants until you can feel they will come up easily, or the roots will break.

Salsify can be kept for a couple of days in the salad compartment of the fridge, but it's best to dig them up as you need them.

Cooking with salsify

Salsify can be boiled or mashed, added to cold dishes or eaten hot as a second vegetable. They can also be added to soups, stews, casseroles and curries.

BOILED OR STEAMED SALSIFY
Scrub thoroughly or peel salsify roots and cut into regular lengths. Steam or simmer gently until tender. Drain well and return to the pan with a little butter and chopped fresh herbs. Stir gently and serve hot.

ONE-POT MEALS
Scrub roots or peel and cut into lengths or slices. Add to casseroles, stews and curries as well as chilli and bolognese dishes to add bulk.

MASHED
Scrub roots and steam or simmer gently until soft. Drain well, then mash with a little butter and stir in a few chopped fresh herbs if liked.

FRITTERS
Scrub or peel roots and steam for about 30 minutes until tender. Mash roughly and stir in 2 tbsp of Greek yoghurt, 2 tbsp of cream and 2 tbsp of corn flour.

Season with a little salt and black pepper, if preferred. Drop spoonfuls of the mixture into a frying pan or skillet with a little hot oil and cook for a few minutes on each side. Remove from pan and drain on kitchen paper. Serve hot or cold.

SALSIFY AND EGGS
Scrub roots thoroughly or peel them and cut into chunky pieces. Steam or bring to the boil and simmer until tender. Drain well and cool. When cooled, put into a bowl or serving dish and gently stir in chopped boiled eggs. Serve as it is, or add a white sauce. Béchamel, cheese or mushroom sauces all work well. Garnish with a sprig of parsley or chopped chives.

POTATOES

About potatoes
Potatoes don't need any introduction as they have been a staple food of many countries for generations. In recent years, with diet fads and celebrity dress sizes, potatoes have had a bad 'carb' press. We do however need carbohydrates in a balanced diet and potatoes are perfect for that. Although they are a carbohydrate, they have a high mineral and vitamin content, unlike white bread or pasta.

Additives, such as oils and sauces add to the fat and calorie intake, but with fresh home grown potatoes, you won't want to add anything to spoil the perfect potato taste.

In generations past, people believed we could live on the humble spud alone, although the Irish potato famine brought home just how fragile that kind of dependence can be. Potatoes are an important part of our diet but shouldn't be eaten to the exclusion of everything else!

Properties of potatoes

As well as being a healthy carbohydrate, potatoes are a good source of vitamin C, B vitamins and minerals – lots of good reasons to include the potato in our everyday diets.

Potatoes have been used in medicinal preparations over many generations as a digestive aid, and also as a poultice for skin sores. The leaves, stems and fruits of the potato plant are poisonous and, because of this, potatoes have had a bad press in the past. However, the tubers (potatoes) that grow underground are a great source of wholesome goodness.

Growing potatoes

In days gone by, vegetable growers would plant just a piece of potato or even peelings to start another crop. This method does work but the plants are more susceptible to blight and other disease. The seed potatoes available in garden centres have been grown at high altitude and have a resistance to blight, although there is never any guarantee your plants won't suffer.

Blight tends to attack when the weather is warm and muggy. Some potato growers spray regularly with a 'Bordeaux' mix to prevent attacks. A Bordeaux mix is a combination of hydrated lime and copper sulphate and is available at most large garden centres.

Seed potatoes need to 'sprout' before planting. Place them in a box in single layers in a dark place until they have produced a sprout or two.

Early crop potatoes can be started before Christmas and should be ready to eat around Easter time. They will need protecting from the cold though and should be planted under cloches or in polytunnels.

Main crop potatoes should be planted around Easter time and will be fully developed by late summer.

There are a number of different ways to grow potatoes and, with specially made containers on the market these days, you don't even need a vegetable patch to produce a good crop. Use a potato barrel and follow the recommendations that come with the container. Old rubber car tyres can be used as well. Some growers are concerned that the chemicals in the rubber may leak into the soil, but there doesn't seem to be any hard evidence of that so far.

Pile two or three tyres on top of each other and fill with fresh compost. Don't mix fresh fertiliser or manure into the soil. Plant seed potatoes about 6 in (15 cm) deep. Early potatoes can be grown in this way, as the tyres keep the soil warm enough for them to develop, although a plastic or glass cover should be placed across the top of the tyres to protect your plants during cold weather.

Traditionally potatoes have been grown in lines and 'earthed up' every couple of weeks (see overleaf). The best crop of potatoes will grow in well-prepared soil and, although this way of growing potatoes is labour intensive to begin with, you will get better results.

Potatoes and tomatoes shouldn't be planted near each other. They belong to the same family and will share diseases.

Potatoes growing in rubber tyres

Choose a fairly sunny, well-drained spot and dig over the ground as deep as you can. Remove any non-organic debris, perennial weeds and large stones. Dig a trench to a depth of around 8 in (20 cm). Some varieties may need a little more depth. Check on the growing recommendations before you start for your particular variety. Tools can be bought or obtained for this job, although a simple spade will suffice.

When the seed potatoes have sprouted, lay them in the prepared trench allowing about 12 in (30 cm) between each one. Place them with the sprouts facing up as far as you can.

Comfrey leaves are a good tonic for the ground. If you have some available in the garden, lay the leaves in the trench and then place the seed potatoes on top of them.

Allow at least 2 ft (60 cm) between rows. Cover the potatoes with the soil you dug out to create the trench. Water well. Pull out any weeds that come up and keep the ground damp, but not waterlogged.

When the potato plants appear, they need 'earthing up' in order to keep the growing potatoes covered up – any exposed to the light will become green and poisonous. Using a rake, carefully draw soil from both sides of each line to cover the new plants. Firm the soil on either side of the ridge and water. Repeat after a couple of weeks when the plants are beginning to show above the surface again. And then do it once more a few weeks later. After three times of earthing up your potatoes, you can leave them alone to get on with growing. Water well in dry periods and keep the weeds away, and you should get a good crop.

Steal a few new potatoes as a treat in the summer months. Use your hands to scrape away the earth from the sides of the ridge around your plants and choose a few baby potatoes. Push the soil back over the roots afterwards.

Use potatoes from the end of the summer or when the plants start dying back. Harvest the whole crop before autumn. If they are left in wet ground, potatoes will rot. Dig up every plant carefully using a fork, allowing a large area around each plant. Lay the potatoes on dry ground in the sun for a few hours. Turn over every now and again. Bring them in at night. If they are left too long in the sun they will become green and inedible, so just a few hours to dry them is enough.

Store in single layers in cardboard boxes or specially designed potato containers. Keep out of damp and direct light and they will last several months.

Cooking with potatoes

Potatoes are one of the most versatile vegetables on the planet. They can be used in so many ways it would be difficult to list them all in one book, let alone a chapter. Here are a few ideas to fire your imagination in the kitchen.

Potatoes from your own garden shouldn't need peeling, only very light scrubbing. Fresh potatoes out of the ground have very fine skins and can often be rubbed off and rinsed. If the skin has not 'set', the potatoes aren't very suitable for 'jacket potatoes' but they can be used in every other way.

There are literally thousands of seed potatoes you can grow at home, although some varieties will be better suited to mash rather than roasts for example. 'Maris Piper' are a versatile all-rounder and are especially good for making chips. 'King Edwards' are a classic roast potato and are the traditional variety to serve at Christmas. 'Vivaldi' are perfect for boiling or mashing. To make a good choice of seed potato, it's best to scan online the varieties available (Thompson & Morgan have a great selection) or ask for advice at your local garden centre.

BOILED POTATOES

Prepare your potatoes as above and cut into fairly small pieces. Place in a pan and cover with water. Bring to the boil, then reduce heat and simmer until the potatoes are tender right through. They can also be steamed. Prepare in the same way and place in the steamer for around 20 minutes or until cooked. Drain well.

Once boiled, potatoes can be used in a variety of ways:

MASH

Mash boiled potatoes with a little butter and milk. Stir in a few chopped fresh herbs if liked. Mashed potatoes can be served hot with many everyday meals. Use to cover a mince and tomato dish to make a cottage or shepherd's pie.

BUBBLE AND SQUEAK

Bubble and squeak is an old English dish made with leftover mashed potato and cooked cabbage or spring greens. Chop the cabbage or greens finely and mix with mashed potatoes. If the mixture is dry, stir in a beaten egg or a little milk. Form into burger shapes and fry in a pan with a little heated cooking oil, or use a non-stick frying pan or skillet.

Instead of mashing your boiled potatoes, they can be boiled and used in other ways:

POTATO SALAD

Cut prepared potatoes into regular-sized pieces and boil or steam until just cooked. Drain and leave to cool. When cold put the potato pieces into a bowl with a few chopped spring onions or shallots. Stir in a dressing made with half mayonnaise and half natural yoghurt, or use your preferred dressing. Chill before serving and garnish with a few chopped chives or a sprig of parsley.

GARLIC POTATOES

Cut prepared potatoes into quarter or half inch slices and boil or steam for about 10 minutes or until just cooked. Drain well and layer into an ovenproof dish. Add some crushed garlic cloves and a few chopped fresh herbs in between the layers. Pour over some warmed milk to about halfway up the dish and cook in a medium oven (Gas Mark 4, 350°F or 180°C) for about 20 minutes until hot right through. Grate some cheese and sprinkle over the top of the potatoes. Grill under a medium grill for a few minutes to brown off. Serve hot.

JACKET POTATOES

Choose medium to large potatoes with as few blemishes as possible. Scrub and bake in the oven until cooked through. Potatoes can be cut in half, sprinkled with grated cheese and browned under a grill. Or scoop out the flesh after cooking and mix in a bowl with tuna, cheese, ham, beans or whatever you have available. Mix the potato well with your choice of filling and spoon mixture back into the skins. Put back into the oven to re-heat. If you are re-heating meat or fish make sure it is piping hot right through before serving.

SNACKS

Potato skins can be sprinkled with a little sea salt and baked in a hot oven. Potatoes can also be cut and fried to make homemade chips or crisps, or baked as wedges.

ROAST POTATOES

Prepare and cut potatoes into fairly large pieces and boil for about 5 or 10 minutes. Drain and put onto an oven tray or around a Sunday roast. Cook for about 45 minutes to an hour, turning from time to time.

There really are hundreds of ways to serve potatoes and using homegrown ones will make your meals even tastier.

CHAPTER 3

EVERYDAY VEG

Peas and beans have been traditional everyday vegetables for generations and they are easy to grow, eat and store.

Broccoli has had much media coverage over the last few years and is now known as a 'super-food'. It is also easy to grow and if you get it right, your plants will keep cropping for many months.

This chapter covers five main everyday vegetables that can be served with just about any meal:

- peas

- beans

- broccoli

- asparagus

- courgettes.

As well as being a 'second veg', all of these vegetables can be used as the main ingredient in particularly tasty dishes that ordinarily you may not consider everyday meals but are in fact just as simple as throwing a few fish fingers under the grill – well almost.

Although asparagus is usually considered to be a luxury vegetable, probably due to the price, it is in fact a great crop to grow in your garden. The benefits are enormous and as it's a perennial crop it comes back year after year. There isn't much maintenance involved either.

Courgettes have been grown in the UK for many years. We used to let them grow into full-sized marrows, but courgette hybrids these days will give a tasty crop of courgettes that you will want to eat before they swell into a rather bland marrow. Courgettes can be used in many dishes from ratatouille to a simple stir-fry.

All five of the everyday vegetables included in this chapter will grow successfully in a moderate climate with the right conditions and a little TLC.

PEAS

About peas

Peas have been cultivated for human consumption for thousands of years as a valuable dried food crop. It wasn't until a couple of hundred years ago that they were eaten as a fresh vegetable. Dried peas can be stored almost indefinitely, and were used on long sea voyages for crew and passengers alike where other foods perished.

As soon as the pea became a vegetable popular in the kitchen garden, cross-breeding began and nowadays we have many different varieties. The *mange tout* or sugar snap pea is eaten whole before the pea inside the pod starts to develop. These peas are excellent for snacks and salads. Then there are various sizes right through to the large 'marrowfat' types that are often used to make mushy peas and added to slow-cooked dishes.

Peas freeze well and with the relatively inexpensive frozen peas on the market, they have taken a back seat in the kitchen garden over the past 20 or 30 years. Although growing them yourself may not seem cost effective, they are a fun crop to grow and there is nothing like the taste of home produce. Children get involved in shelling peas quite happily and that in itself is a worthy reason to grow them yourself.

Properties of peas

Peas are a good source of vitamins A and C, both of which help neutralise free radicals. There is some evidence to support the fact that peas can help alleviate symptoms of age-related ailments. They contain B vitamins which boost the immune system and help keep the body strong and resistant to disease. They also contain significant amounts of niacin (vitamin B3), which helps the body to absorb iron.

Growing peas

Growing peas isn't a difficult process but it's worth arming yourself with the right information and equipment before you get started. Peas are normally a climbing plant, although you may find a hybrid variety that will grow as a small shrub. To support your climbing plants you will need some sort of trellis or fencing.

If your garden fence is facing south and gets a lot of sun, use the fence as a support. Attach a few strings horizontally every 6 in (15 cm) or so, and help the plants along by curling them round the strings as they grow. Pea plants send out tendrils, which enable them to cling on ferociously. Peas will happily use anything as a support frame, so keep an eye on surrounding plants.

They can also be grown along borders, although they will need support. Chicken wire or pig wire stretched across an area between posts is a good system. Make sure the posts or wire don't blow down in the wind. Pea netting is available from garden centres.

For shorter growing plants, pea sticks can be used successfully. Collect fairly straight branches from trees with a branch or two leading off each one for the plants to cling to. Last year's raspberry canes are very usable if tree branches aren't easy to find. Alternatively, buy pea supports from a garden centre.

Choose a sunny and well-drained spot in the garden. Although peas are a cool growing crop, they will need all the light they can get in the early stages of development, and again when the fruits mature. Peas and beans grow well together and, if you have the space, a 'pea and bean' patch is ideal.

As soon as the ground is workable in early spring, dig over and remove any perennial weeds, non-organic debris and large stones. Peas are usually planted early in the year as they are a cool growing crop. Check your seed packet for the manufacturer's growing recommendations for your particular variety. If possible, work the ground in the previous autumn and cover with an organic mulch. Dig over lightly before planting peas in late winter or early spring.

Pea plant

Once preparations are made for your pea patch, it's time to sow the seed. The seed you are planting is simply a dried pea. They are easy to handle and can be sown every couple of inches along a row.

Sow as close as possible to the pea support system you have in place. Make a trench about 1.5–2 in (3–5 cm) deep and place one pea seed every 2 in (5 cm) along the row. Cover the seeds with soil and water gently. Allow enough space between rows to maintain and harvest your crops.

Some growers prefer to soak seed in water for a few hours before sowing to encourage faster germination and, in days gone past, gardeners in rural areas would soak seed in paraffin to deter birds and mice. If birds or mice are a problem in your garden, cover with a wildlife-friendly netting until the seeds germinate.

Peas should come up within a couple of weeks and, all being well, will get on with the business of growing all by themselves. Water your plants if the ground is dry but never over water. Because peas are an early crop, they will normally get enough water from the natural rainfall.

In good conditions you can almost watch pea plants grow. They will cling on to their support system and within a few months begin to produce flowers. When they first start growing they may need a little help to find the support system. Gently ease the tendrils round the sticks or netting.

From the flowers the fruits – pods – are produced. If you are growing sugar snap or *mange tout* varieties, pick as soon as the pods are a couple of inches long. They are sweet and tender at this size and become too coarse if left too long.

Everyday garden peas should be picked when there are obviously developed peas in the pods. Larger marrowfat peas will take longer to mature.

Peas can be left to dry on the plants and can be collected for using in the winter months, or for sowing the following year. Make sure peas are completely dry before storing. Keep in jars in a dry place out of direct light until required.

When your plants have died back, leave them in the ground until they have completely shrivelled and then dig into the soil. Pea plants capture nitrogen from the air and store it in their root system. Digging the plants back into the soil will replenish nitrogen and benefit next year's crops.

Eating peas

Peas have been a valuable dried food crop for many generations and they are a perfect store cupboard ingredient for the winter months.

SALADS AND COLD DISHES

Sugar snap or *mange tout* peas can be added whole or chopped into salads. The sweet flavour is perfect with a chopped green salad. These varieties of peas are also great snacks for children. Serve them as a side dish tossed lightly in olive oil or a walnut salad dressing for a special treat.

Cooking with peas

FRESH GARDEN PEAS

Shell peas and boil or steam until tender. Toss in a little melted butter and chopped mint and serve hot.

MUSHY PEAS

Mushy peas are very popular in many parts of the UK, particularly the north of England. Made from large marrowfat peas, the recipe is simple to make at home. In a large heavy-based saucepan, cover marrowfat peas with water and bring to the boil. Add a little salt and sugar if liked. Reduce the heat and simmer until peas are soft and 'mushy'. Chopped mint or other fresh herbs can be added to spice up the flavour. Drain peas and mash until smooth. Serve hot.

CASSEROLES AND STEWS
Peas can be added to casseroles and stews. Fresh peas take a little longer to cook than bought frozen peas and should be added to your recipe at least 20 minutes before the end of cooking time.

PEA SOUP
Gently heat 2 oz (50 g) of butter or a little oil in a heavy-based pan and cook a finely chopped onion until soft. Stir to prevent burning. Add 2 lb (900 g) of shelled fresh peas with a handful of chopped mint and 2 pt (1.1 l) of chicken or vegetable stock. Bring to the boil then reduce the heat and simmer until peas are tender. Remove from the heat and allow to cool for about 10 minutes. Liquidise in a food processor or blender then return to the pan and heat through gently, stirring to prevent burning. Serve hot with crusty bread.

PEA GUACAMOLE
Peas can be used in place of avocado for this tasty dip. Steam or boil about 12 oz (350 g) of shelled peas until tender. Drain and leave to cool. Put into a food processor or blender with one or two cloves of crushed garlic, two finely sliced spring onions (or one chopped shallot), a handful of chopped fresh coriander, 1 tbsp of olive or nut oil, seasoning, and a little grated rind and the juice of a lemon or lime. Blend until smooth and chill for 30 minutes before serving.

BEANS

About beans
Beans have been cultivated for home use since around the sixteenth century although it wasn't until the turn of the twentieth century that 'stringless'

varieties were available to the home gardener. French beans, or bush beans, grow quickly and produce good crops without too much trouble.

Beans are best eaten whole before the bean inside the pod develops, although some can be left to mature and stored for winter use or sown the following year.

There are literally hundreds of different beans available for the home gardener to grow, although the basic French bean and runner bean are the most popular varieties and tend to crop well.

Properties of beans

Beans are a good source of vitamins A and C and can be safely eaten every day, but should always be cooked before consumption. Raw beans contain hydrocyanic acid, which is poisonous and can cause sickness and blood pressure problems. Once cooked, however, green beans can help reduce high blood pressure.

All green beans contain significant amounts of calcium and dietary fibre as well as folate and protein. The water in which beans are cooked will contain iron and should be used to make gravy or sauces rather than being discarded.

Growing beans

There are hundreds of different types of beans and, if you have the space, it's worthwhile experimenting with a few different varieties. French or bush beans take up little space in the garden and can be grown as a border plant. They are quick to grow and can be planted at regular intervals throughout the spring and summer months. Climbing varieties, such as runner beans need a little more attention but the taste is definitely worth the extra effort.

Generally beans need a sunny spot to develop well, although different varieties have different growing needs and it's best to check the manufacturer's growing recommendations before you decide on the right place. Peas and beans grow well together.

In a well-drained and sunny spot, dig the ground over and remove any perennial weeds, non-organic debris and large stones. Rake over to level the ground.

If you are planting climbing beans such as runner beans, they will need a support system to climb up. Many gardeners use a tepee method. Firmly place canes (6–8 ft long) into the ground in a circle and tie the tops together with garden twine to form a tepee shape. Run strings around the outside of the canes at 8–12 in (20–30 cm) intervals, wrapping twine around the canes to keep them in place. Alternatively a simple chicken or pig wire structure can be used. Always make sure the support structure is firmly pushed into the ground to avoid damage in high winds. If the structure blows down, the plants will suffer.

Beans can be planted directly outside in late spring, after all danger of frost has passed. They are a fast growing plant and won't need an early start in the greenhouse.

Bean plant

Make a shallow trench (about an inch deep) as close as possible to the support you have in place. Plant your beans around the outside of the circle if you are using the tepee method and place individual beans every 2–3 in (5–6 cm). Cover with soil and water well. Sow French beans in lines, allowing 6–12 in (15–30 cm) between plants. Check on your seed packet for variations.

Beans love water but should never be allowed to become waterlogged. In hot dry periods, runner bean flowers should be 'set' by spraying with water at least once a day, preferably twice, or the flowers will drop off the plant and the beans won't develop.

Keep watered and weed-free, and your beans should grow well. As soon as you spot the young beans, start picking and eating, especially with French bean varieties. They crop well and it will be hard to keep up with them. Pick them and give some away or freeze some if necessary. A few may be left on the plants for planting next year. Decide on a few early beans to leave as they take a long time to reach maturity. Store in a dark dry place for planting the following year.

When the plants have finished cropping, pull up and compost. Excess beans should be frozen quickly. They freeze well, but some of the texture and a little of the taste will be lost in freezing. Green beans will keep for a few days in the fridge or cold place after picking.

Cooking with beans

Prepare green beans by topping and tailing to remove stalks. Runner beans should be topped, tailed and sliced before cooking. Small green beans can often be left whole or cut into two or three pieces. Always use beans that are not stringy, where possible. If runner beans have grown quite large, they may be a little stringy, but when removing the top of the bean you should be able to pull the strings from the sides with ease.

Beans should always be cooked thoroughly before eating as they contain a poison in their raw state. Cooking neutralises the problem and they can be safely eaten once cooked.

Beans can be cooled and eaten cold after cooking, and added to any cold dish. French or runner beans are particularly good to mix into a green salad. The larger beans such as butter beans and flageolet beans are also excellent salad ingredients.

GREEN BEAN SALAD

Cook the beans until tender, drain and set aside until completely cold. Arrange lettuce leaves, young spinach leaves and watercress in a serving dish. When the beans are cold, mix gently in a bowl with black olives and crumbled feta cheese. Place the bean mixture on a bed of leaves and pour over a little olive or nut oil, or use a vinaigrette dressing. Garnish with a handful of chopped chives. Chill for 10 minutes and serve.

GARLIC BEANS

Cook the beans until tender and drain. In a wok or large frying pan heat a little oil and cook a couple of chopped garlic cloves for a minute or two. Add the beans and some chopped basil and stir gently until thoroughly re-heated. Serve hot.

BLACK PEPPERED BEANS

Runner beans are perfect for this dish although any green beans will do. Cook beans until tender and drain well. Toss in a little melted butter and freshly ground black pepper. Serve immediately.

BEANS AND BACON

In a large heavy-based pan, heat a little oil or butter and gently cook a chopped onion. Stir until the onion begins to soften. Add about 1.5 lb (700 g) of cut beans, a teaspoon of fresh thyme and about 100 ml of vegetable, chicken or ham stock. Stir in a couple of rashers of chopped cooked bacon and bring to the boil. Reduce heat and simmer for about 10 or 15 minutes until the beans are tender. Serve hot.

Green beans can be added to soups, stews, casseroles and curry dishes, as well as being a perfect vegetable to serve with your favourite Sunday roast.

BROCCOLI

About broccoli

Broccoli is a member of the brassica family and, although many varieties of brassica have been consumed since ancient times, broccoli wasn't cultivated until the sixteenth century. It started off as a garden vegetable in Italy but took a few hundred years until it reached all corners of Europe and America. In the UK before the turn of the twentieth century broccoli was considered to be a strange food, but around the beginning of the twentieth century it was finally cultivated commercially and became an everyday vegetable. It is now regarded as one of the super-foods.

There are different varieties of broccoli but generally they will all grow well in a moderate climate, and are a useful and practical addition to the vegetable garden.

Properties of broccoli

Broccoli has become known as a super-food in recent years with good reason. It's packed with vitamins and minerals and is considered to be a powerful anti-oxidant, eliminating free radicals and boosting the immune system.

It has significant quantities of vitamin B5 (pantothenic acid) as well as dietary fibre, and is a vegetable worthy of everyday use. With regard to vitamins and minerals, broccoli doesn't differ that much from the other members of the brassica family such as cabbage and kale, although it is easy to grow and very practical to cook with as it needs little preparation. It can also be tastier than other brassicas.

Purple-sprouting broccoli is higher in anti-oxidants and an attractive alternative to regular varieties.

Growing broccoli

Brassicas, including all broccoli varieties, won't thrive in an acidic soil. If your soil has a high level of acid, incorporate lime into the soil before planting. It's also a good idea to dig in plenty of well-rotted manure or organic fertiliser during the autumn or winter before.

Broccoli prefers a sunny position but will tolerate part shade. Choose a spot that's out of wind tunnels or frost pockets as plants will keep growing late in the year. Dig over the ground and remove any perennial weeds and non-organic debris. Although broccoli is a fairly hardy plant, it likes a good clean soil to thrive and crop well. The area must also be well drained.

Broccoli seed generally needs to be kept warm during the germination period and therefore they are best started off in a greenhouse or conservatory or other warm place indoors. Check on the manufacturer's sowing recommendations on your seed packet, but usually broccoli seed is sown in early spring.

Fill well-drained seed trays with fresh compost and sow seed fairly thinly. Label the trays, especially if you are growing other brassica plants, as they all look very similar in the early stages of growth and can be difficult to tell apart. Keep warm and watered until plants have three or four true leaves, not counting the first two.

Broccoli plant

Broccoli can be planted outside in a seedbed a little later in the year but may need protecting with a cloche or similar covering overnight.

When your seedlings are ready to plant out, water the compost well before removing them from the trays. Handle as little as possible and try not to touch the roots too much as any root damage could affect the growth of the plant. Plant out in a prepared bed allowing about 18–24 in (45–60 cm) between plants and around 2 ft (60 cm) between rows. Double-check on your seed packet for variations.

Weed regularly and water often, especially in dry periods. Watch out for cabbage white butterfly attacks. It's always nice to see butterflies in the garden but the cabbage white butterfly will lay its eggs on the underside of brassica leaves. When the caterpillars hatch out they can devour whole plants before you even notice they are there.

If you see cabbage white butterflies hovering around your broccoli patch, the following morning check on the underside of the leaves and destroy any eggs that are laid there. Remove the leaf if necessary or scrape the eggs off gently – but do get rid of them. Planting strong smelling herbs close by sometimes deters the butterfly but don't rely on it.

When plants start producing the flower heads, cut with a sharp knife and eat them. Don't wait for the heads to get large as they may turn to flowers very quickly. Generally for the home grower, it's best to remove this first stalk which encourages others to follow. This will mean many small broccoli heads rather than one large one, but the plants will keep producing for longer and the smaller the stalks the tastier they are.

Broccoli will also grow in containers or large pots as long as they are well drained but not allowed to dry out.

Cut broccoli as often as you can. If you have too much to eat, it will keep for a couple of days in the fridge or break into small florets and freeze quickly on trays. Broccoli will keep for many months in a freezer. Remember to label the container or freezer bag before storing.

Eating broccoli

Broccoli can be eaten raw although most people find the taste rather too strong. A few very tiny florets broken off a larger head of broccoli can be mixed into a salad bowl. This results in a nutty flavour and makes an interesting addition to a regular green salad, without being overpowering in taste.

Generally, though, broccoli is cooked but shouldn't be overcooked. Steam or boil until just tender.

Cooking with broccoli

BROCCOLI AND CHEESE

Boil or steam broccoli until just cooked. Drain well and put into an ovenproof dish. Then make a cheese sauce. Melt 1 oz (25 g) of butter in a small pan. Add 1 oz (25 g) of flour and stir well, cooking for a few seconds over a low heat. Stir in about half a pint (300 ml) of milk very slowly to avoid lumps forming.

Cook over a low heat, stirring all the time until the sauce starts to thicken. Remove from the heat and stir in about 2 oz (50 g) of grated cheese, until melted. Pour the sauce over the broccoli and heat through in the oven for about 15 minutes or put under a medium grill to brown. Serve hot.

BROCCOLI AND FENNEL SOUP

Bring a large pan of vegetable or chicken stock to the boil. Finely chop a fennel bulb and add to the stock. Bring back to the boil, reduce heat and simmer for about 10 minutes. Break florets from three large broccoli heads, or the equivalent in smaller heads. Cut broccoli stems into thin slices and add all to the pan with about 3 tbsp of chopped fresh sage. Bring back to the boil again, reduce heat and simmer until all vegetables are tender. Remove from heat and allow to cool for a while. Blend in a liquidiser or food processor and return to the pan. Gently re-heat for a few minutes until hot right through, stirring all the time to prevent burning. Serve hot with crusty bread or croutons.

BROCCOLI QUICHE

Buy or make shortcrust pastry. To make your own pastry, cut 3 oz (75 g) of butter or margarine into small cubes and rub, with your fingertips, into 6 oz (150 g) of flour until the mixture resembles fine breadcrumbs. Stir in a little water at a time and push the pastry together with your hands or a palette knife until a dough is formed. Don't add too much water as it will become sticky. If this does happen, however, a little extra flour may help. Roll out the pastry on a floured board and cut to fit your baking tin. Place in the lightly greased tin, lining the sides and bottom.

Place a circle of greaseproof paper on top of the pastry and throw in a few dried beans. Bake 'blind' in a preheated oven, Gas Mark 6, 400°F or 200°C, for about 10–15 minutes until the pastry is set. Remove the beans and greaseproof paper.

While the pastry is cooking, steam or boil a handful of broccoli florets, broken into small pieces. Drain well and cool for ten minutes. Lay cooked broccoli onto the pastry case. Spread 4 oz (100 g) of grated cheese on top. In a bowl, beat two eggs and mix with 5 fl oz (150 ml) of milk or single cream. Season with a little salt and black pepper.

Pour the egg mixture on top of the broccoli and cheese and cook in the pre-heated oven for around 30 minutes until set and golden brown. Serve hot or cold with a green salad.

ASPARAGUS

About asparagus

Asparagus is often considered to be a luxury food, probably because of the price we pay for it in the shops. Asparagus is in fact a very practical crop to grow in the home vegetable garden. It is available before most other summer vegetables are ready and is also a perennial crop that will keep coming back every year. With a little TLC plants will grow and provide more asparagus than you and your family could possibly eat!

Asparagus is indigenous to coastal areas and thrives with seaweed fertilisers and dressings. It was documented by the Romans, who prized it as a medicinal as well as a culinary vegetable. There are records of asparagus being cultivated in ancient Egyptian times, although it didn't become a popular cultivated vegetable in Europe and America until the sixteenth century.

Properties of asparagus

Asparagus is a nutritious vegetable and is said to have many medicinal qualities. High in vitamins and minerals, it is a worthy vegetable to add to your everyday diet. It is low in calories and is also believed to help alleviate symptoms of kidney disorders. It can be safely eaten raw as well as cooked.

Asparagus helps cancel water retention in the body and the water in which asparagus is cooked makes a healthy and nutritious drink.

Asparagus is one of the few garden vegetables with a significant quantity of vitamin E, which is more often found in nuts and seeds.

Growing asparagus

One thing that puts a lot of people off growing asparagus is that you have to wait for three years or more before the spears can be used if you grow from seed, and a full crop won't be available for five years. However, asparagus 'crowns' can be bought in garden centres and will be ready to use in the year after planting, if you buy three-year-old crowns.

If you decide to plant your asparagus from seed, it is definitely more satisfying but you will have to look after the plants until they are ready to be harvested. Read through the manufacturer's growing recommendations on the seed packet for exact instructions for your variety and region.

Three-year-old crowns should be bought from a reputable supplier and, if they come with any special instructions, read before planting. Male crowns are better if you can find them. Female crowns have to put energy into developing seed so won't produce as many spears as male plants.

Asparagus is a perennial and a healthy plant will last many years. A permanent patch should be given over to them as they are better left in one place rather than disturbed. Because they will stay in the same place for the foreseeable future, the more you prepare before planting, the better.

The soil should have a pH of 6.5 to 7.5 and it is worth testing your soil before planting the crowns. Once you have all the elements in order, asparagus plants will crop for 15 years or more, so it's well worth getting the balance right to begin with.

Asparagus plants

Asparagus thrives in full sun so a sunny position should be chosen, although the plants will get fairly tall after they have finished cropping each year so care should be taken that they don't over shadow other plants. A raised bed system on the northern side of your garden is ideal if possible. It must be a well-drained spot.

Dig over the ground as deeply as you can and remove any perennial weeds, non-organic debris and large stones. Incorporate sand or any other products you need to get the pH balance right and add as much fertiliser as you can. Asparagus is native to coastal areas and thrives in a soil rich with seaweed and sand additives.

During the spring or whenever the crowns are available, plant about 6 in (15 cm) deep and allow 12–18 in (30–45 cm) between plants. Cover crowns with a mixture of soil and sand. Water well but don't compact the soil. After a couple of weeks, asparagus will start showing through, but should not be cut in the first year. Keep free of weeds and watered during hot dry weather and allow the plants to produce ferns and die back on their own.

Early in the following spring, cut down the ferns. Wear gloves when you do this as they can be sharp. In subsequent years, ferns should be cut down in the autumn and a layer of seaweed spread over the whole area. Any un-rotted material should be removed in the spring. Then add sand and soil to increase the height of the bed. Asparagus crowns will grow bigger every year and the bed will need raising to accommodate them.

During the second year, harvest the spears when they are around 6 in (15 cm) or so, by cutting with a sharp knife as close to the surface of the soil as possible. Cut early in the morning and rinse under very cold water to prevent the spears from becoming limp. Keep harvesting until around mid-June or when the plants start producing ferns.

In late summer or early autumn, asparagus beetle can attack. Watch out for them and pick them off or treat with an organic product to get rid of them. They won't kill the plant, but the crop will be reduced the following year. Cutting back the ferns will help deter them.

To produce your own asparagus seed, leave the ferns to grow if you have female plants and allow them to develop seed. Collect the seed when fully ripe and sow in well-drained trays of compost until they have germinated. Transplant them into pots and look after them for a couple of years before putting out into the garden. Don't cut the spears in the first three or four years though as this will weaken the plants.

Although this all sounds rather involved and time consuming, once the plants have become established, very little maintenance is required and the asparagus spears you harvest year after year will be well worth the effort.

Eating asparagus

Asparagus comes early in the year when other vegetables are just getting started in the garden, so they are always a welcome addition to the dinner table, and can be eaten cooked or raw.

ASPARAGUS SALADS

A few young spears of raw asparagus cut in half are a nutritious and tasty addition to the salad bowl. Or make an asparagus side salad. Cut a few fresh asparagus spears in short lengths and mix in some chopped nuts and a light dressing of nut oil. Chill for 20 or 30 minutes before serving.

Cooking with asparagus

Asparagus can be lightly boiled or steamed to accompany almost any meal. When just cooked, drain well and toss in a little butter. Avoid over-cooking. Experiment with adding a few chopped fresh herbs or black pepper if liked. Stir in after cooking.

ASPARAGUS OMELETTE

Steam or lightly boil asparagus spears until just cooked. Drain well and cut into short lengths, keeping two or three whole spears aside per omelette. Beat two eggs per person in a bowl and add grated cheese or crumbled feta cheese to taste. Season with salt and black pepper (optional).

Heat a little sunflower oil in a frying pan and pour in the egg mixture. Cook on a low heat for a couple of minutes, then add asparagus pieces on top. When the underside of the omelette is cooked, turn over, or fold in half and turn over. Then cook gently until the eggs are set. Remove from the pan and serve on a warm plate, garnished with whole asparagus spears. Serve hot with a green salad.

ASPARAGUS SOUP

This recipe is for a basic asparagus soup but other vegetables can be added if you have them available. Melt 3 oz (75 g) of butter or a low fat equivalent in a large heavy-based saucepan. Cut about 1 lb (450 g) of asparagus spears into small pieces and add to the pan with one or two chopped onions. Cook on a low heat for a few minutes until the vegetables begin to soften, stirring to prevent burning.

Add 2 pints (1 litre) of vegetable or chicken stock and bring to the boil. Add some salt, black pepper and chopped fresh herbs to taste. Reduce the heat and simmer for about 40 minutes until the asparagus and onions are tender. Serve hot with crusty bread or croutons.

This recipe can be blended in a food processor or liquidiser if a creamy soup is preferred. After cooking, cool for about 10 minutes then blend until smooth. Return the soup to the pan and re-heat gently, stirring all the time. Add a swirl of single cream to individual bowls of soup for an extra special treat.

COURGETTES

About courgettes

Courgettes (or zucchini) didn't become a popular vegetable in Europe and America until the early twentieth century, although marrows had been grown for many years before that. Although marrows are nutritious and a useful kitchen garden vegetable to grow, they are nowhere near as tasty as the young courgettes.

Courgettes are part of the very large squash family, which also includes pumpkins, cucumbers, and so on. Many of the squash vegetables originated in America, but courgettes became popular in the Mediterranean area, when the

Italians started eating young immature marrows. They then became a vegetable in their own right. Courgettes will grow in a moderate climate and only need a little extra protection if started off early in the year.

Properties of courgettes

Courgettes are a good source of niacin (vitamin B3) and other vitamins, including vitamin A. The seeds have a mixture of natural chemicals that have been found to help reduce enlargement of the prostate gland, which is a common condition in men aged over 50.

Courgettes are a good source of folate, potassium and manganese and are very low in calories. Plants can produce an overwhelming number of fruits, and are often given away during the growing season. Courgette flowers are also a nutritious delicacy. The flowers are short-lived and not easy to transport, making them an expensive food to buy.

Growing courgettes

Courgettes are probably one of the easiest vegetables to grow. There are a number of interesting varieties to grow in the home vegetable garden. The regular courgette resembles a cucumber but there are different shapes and colours available from most garden suppliers.

Courgette plants are very similar to most squash plants in the early stages of development and, if you are growing pumpkins and cucumbers as well as courgettes, remember to label the seed trays or pots, as it's almost impossible to tell the difference between seedlings.

Choose a sunny well-drained spot in the garden. Courgettes will tolerate partial shade, but double-check on the manufacturer's growing recommendations on your seed packet for variations. Some growers like to plant squash plants on a ridge or mound. Courgettes often come up on their own in a compost heap.

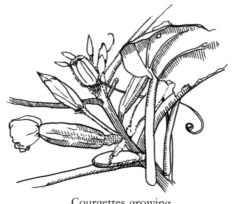

Courgettes growing

Dig over the ground and remove any perennial weeds and non-organic debris.

Start courgette seed off in the spring in a greenhouse, conservatory or indoors in a bright spot. Prepare well-drained pots with fresh compost and sow two seeds per pot. If both seeds germinate, remove the weaker one and leave the other to grow on. Biodegradable pots can be used to avoid damaging roots when transplanting, although courgettes are fairly hardy and, as long as the roots aren't over-handled, they should transplant without harm.

Keep your pots watered, but never waterlogged, and in a warm place until all danger of frost has passed and the plants have at least three or four true leaves. Because courgettes grow rapidly, it's worth sowing just a few early in the year and then sowing seed directly outside a little later.

Transplant courgettes to your prepared bed in the morning of a warm sunny day, ideally. Soak the pots with water before removing the plants. Tip the whole contents of the pot out gently and try not to handle the roots too much.

Plant out allowing 18–24 in (45–60 cm) per plant. This seems like a huge space for such small plants but they will grow into it very quickly. Water well after planting and keep weeds away in the early stages of growth. Make sure the plants never dry out and watch out for slug or snail attacks. They can wipe out all your plants in no time, if they get a chance. Use any organic method of slug repellent that you can. Crushed egg shells and sand work well, but will need replacing often, or try old fashioned remedies such as a bowl of beer. Whatever you do, protect your plants from slugs and snails.

In a very short time courgette plants will grow, and slugs and snails will move on to younger plants. The foliage shades the soil around each plant deterring weeds, so once they have become established all you really need to do is make sure they don't dry out.

As soon as the plants start producing courgettes, start using them. Don't wait until they get too big. The plants will crop more and more so you are better off using them while they are small and tastier. Cut through the stalk using a sharp knife, being careful not to damage the plant.

Cooking with courgettes

There are many ways to enjoy courgettes and, if you are growing your own, you'll probably find yourself with so many you will need to get creative in the kitchen.

STIR-FRIES

Cut courgettes into fairly thin slices and add to the other vegetables in the pan. If the peel is a little tough, cook for slightly longer. Young courgettes need very little cooking, just a few minutes in a stir-fry.

ONE-POT MEALS

Cut courgettes into small pieces and add to bolognese or chilli dishes. You can also slice courgettes and place them between layers of lasagne pasta to add bulk; this is especially good in a vegetarian lasagne.

COURGETTES AND HERBS

Courgettes can be served as a side vegetable. Steam or bring to the boil in a saucepan, reduce the heat and simmer until tender. Drain well. Return to the pan and stir in a little butter and chopped fresh herbs of your choice.

COURGETTE PASTA SALAD

Slice four courgettes and put into a pan. Cover with water and bring to the boil. Reduce heat and simmer for about 5 minutes until tender. Remove from the heat, drain and leave to cool completely.

Cook 6 oz (175 g) of pasta shells until just cooked. Drain and put into a large bowl. Stir in a little salad dressing or a light nut oil, then leave to cool.

Roughly chop two medium-sized tomatoes and three or four spring onions. Use two small shallots if spring onions aren't available. When the pasta and courgettes are cold, mix together with the tomatoes and onions. Chill for 10 minutes before serving.

RATATOUILLE

Cut two courgettes into slices and put into a large wok or saucepan with one or two chopped peppers, a chopped onion and three or four large chopped tomatoes. Add more tomatoes if it's too dry. Stir over a low heat until all the vegetables are tender and serve hot.

Aubergine can be added to this dish if you have one. Cut it in half and sprinkle with salt. Leave for about half an hour then rinse off the salt and chop or slice and add to the other ingredients at the beginning of cooking. This everyday dish can be adapted to whatever you have in the fridge. Fresh chopped herbs or spices can be added to taste.

CHEESY COURGETTES

Slice the courgettes. Put them into a pan and cover with water. Bring to the boil, reduce heat and simmer for about 5 minutes or until cooked. Drain well and put into an ovenproof dish. Sprinkle some grated cheese on top and pop into the oven or under a medium grill for a few minutes to brown.

Alternatively, make or buy a cheese or mushroom sauce and pour over the courgettes, then brown off as above.

CHAPTER 4

HERB CORNER

Herbs and spices can transform a simple mince and pasta dish into a delicious lasagne with an Italian flavour, or a simple French loaf into a mouth-watering garlic bread dripping with herbs and butter.

Herbs have been cultivated for thousands of years. Many were used in medicinal preparations, some of which we still use today. During the Middle Ages, herbalists were in danger of being burned at the stake for using what was considered to be magic at the time. Often in such cases, herbs were the perfect remedy for an illness that traditional medicines of the time had failed to treat.

This chapter covers 12 everyday herbs and spices that can be used in the kitchen and for medicinal use:

- basil

- bay

- chives

- coriander

- fennel

- garlic

- mint

- oregano

- parsley

- rosemary

- sage

- thyme.

Herbs are an attractive and practical addition to the garden. Design a herb garden or grow them along pathways or among the flowers and vegetables. The French invented *le potager* to save space in the garden, by growing herbs around small vegetable beds. Many herbs have aromatic and lush foliage and will brighten up any corner of the garden. They also help deter pests and bugs because of their strong scent.

Many herbs are perennial and will come back year after year. A herb garden needs very little maintenance once established.

Most herbs can also be grown in pots and containers, and many can be successfully grown indoors on a sunny windowsill. Herbs should be used regularly to encourage more growth, and more brownie points in the kitchen!

Basil growing

BASIL

About basil

Basil is commonly known as the 'tomato herb' and is an annual plant that needs to be sown every year. Basil has been cultivated for literally thousands of years as a medicinal and culinary herb and many myths and legends are attached to it. It was believed to be the herb of love, attracting your soulmate if a sprig of basil was worn behind the ear.

On a more practical note, however, it is a good fly repellent and a pot of fresh basil near an open window or door in your house will deter flies.

Growing basil

Basil is indigenous to warm regions and won't survive cold temperatures. Start your seeds in a greenhouse, conservatory or a warm place indoors. Sow in well-drained trays or pots of fresh compost. Water regularly but don't allow the compost to become waterlogged.

After all danger of frost has past, and your seedlings are large enough to handle, they can be transplanted out into the garden. Choose a sunny spot, preferably with your tomato plants (so you don't forget to use your basil).

Prepare the ground before planting out by digging over, removing any perennial weeds and raking to a fine tilth. Basil plants are fairly hardy and don't grow very big so can be dotted around the garden wherever you have a space. Check on your seed packet for spacing recommendations for your variety if you are planting out in lines.

Basil likes full sun and drying out can be a problem. Make sure they get plenty of water. Keep weed-free, especially in the early stages of growth, and protect from slugs and snails. Basil isn't normally attractive to pests in the garden, and when established and growing well there shouldn't be any problems.

Basil seed can be planted directly in the garden, but a little later in the year. Check on the recommendations for your particular variety.

Use leaves as soon as the plant is growing well. Pinch out flower heads when they arrive to encourage more leaves. Basil can be successfully grown in pots and containers and is a perfect 'windowsill' herb. Fresh leaves will store for a few days in the fridge, or they can be dried for use in the winter. Hang sprigs upside down in a dark airy room until very dry. Crumble into clean glass jars and label.

Eating basil

Basil is the perfect herb to enhance the taste of tomatoes and will bring the taste of many everyday dishes alive.

- Chop fresh basil leaves finely and sprinkle on pizza before cooking.

- Use a small sprig of basil to garnish any meal.

- Add finely chopped leaves to sauces for pasta dishes or bolognese.

Basil is an excellent herb to add to wine vinegar or oil. Simply add a sprig or two to a bottle of white wine vinegar and leave for a few days to steep before using. Or add to olive oil. Seal the bottle after adding basil and keep in a warm cupboard for a few weeks.

BAY

About bay

Bay is an important culinary herb and is the main ingredient in *bouquet garni*, a mix of herbs that no chef would be without. Bay leaves, in Roman times, were strung into crowns for the victor in physical combat. It has been used as an antiseptic herb but generally is cultivated for culinary use only.

Also known as bay laurel, it is an evergreen shrub, usually grown in containers in more moderate climates. The containers should be kept in a warm place during the winter months if possible. In warmer climates, a bay tree can grow to 15 metres tall.

Bay tree

Growing bay

Bay plants can be started from autumn cuttings or layering branches from an existing plant. To layer a branch, simply pull a long lower branch from a well-established plant to the ground and hold in place with a V-shaped peg. Cover with soil and leave to produce roots. Water gently. During the following year, when the new plant is growing, the original branch can be cut away and the new plant moved.

Cuttings from bay trees should be pushed into compost, cut end down, and watered. Keep in a fairly warm place until roots have developed. The plant can then be transplanted if necessary.

Choose a fairly large well-drained container in which to grow your bay tree. In cold winters it's advisable to bring the plant indoors, so you will need to be able to move it.

During the summer months, bay can often die back through lack of water. The soil in containers and pots dries out quickly and care should be taken to water bay trees regularly. Water very occasionally in the winter, and only when the soil feels dry.

Bay can also be grown from seed although germination rates can be poor. Lay seed on moist compost in a well-drained container and cover with a fine layer of dry compost. Keep in a warm dark place until seedlings appear. Look after seedlings until the plants become large enough to handle and then transplant to their final position in the garden or into their own containers.

The fruits of bay aren't edible but if left to mature they will produce seed.

As with most aromatic herbs, bay rarely suffers from pests and diseases and should thrive for many years with enough heat and water. Re-pot using fresh compost every few years. Keep your containers of bay in a sunny position in the garden or on a patio during the summer.

Eating bay

Bay leaves are waxy in texture and are best removed at the end of the cooking time. Alternatively, they can be dried and crumbled into a dish. They have a slightly bitter taste but compliment many dishes.

- Add a few whole bay leaves to stews and casseroles. Remove before serving.

- Fresh or crumbled dried leaves can also be added to soups and most one-pot meals.

- There is no specific recipe for *bouquet garni* but you can make your own. Using a non-plastic string, tie together sprigs of thyme, parsley and a few bay leaves. Other herbs can be added according to taste, such as celery leaves, tarragon and rosemary. Add the bunch of herbs to your recipe early in the cooking time and remove before serving.

Keep a few dried leaves in a sealed jar for use when the plant is resting during the winter months. Bay tends to have just as much flavour when dried as it does fresh.

CHIVES

About chives

Chives are a member of the onion group and are an easy herb to grow. They are perennial and, once established, will keep growing for many years. Chives grow wild in many parts of Europe and America and have been collected for culinary use for centuries. They originate from China.

Chives growing

Being part of the onion family, they aid digestion and will also help alleviate cold and flu symptoms, although onions are probably more effective as a medicinal aid.

There are a number of different types of chive seed available, including a 'garlic' tasting variety sometimes called Chinese chives. Chive plants produce purple or white flowers, which are edible and can be used as a garnish.

Growing chives

Most plants in the onion family are difficult to germinate from seed. Chives, however, are easy to get going and, once established, a clump of chives will last for many years. They sometimes die back in the winter but will return in the spring. A pot of chives on a windowsill will ensure fresh chives all year round.

Sow seed in well-drained pots or trays of fresh compost and keep watered but not over-watered until seedlings appear. When the plants are big enough to handle they can be transplanted into the garden or individual pots.

Plant out chive plants during the evening when the weather has warmed up, and choose a sunny spot in the garden. In a very hot dry period they may need a little protection from the sun. Chives make an attractive border plant, as well as a useful herb to include in the herb garden. Water the plants well during the summer.

Start using chives when the plant is growing well and looks healthy and strong. Cut with scissors from the outside of each clump, down to about two inches from the ground. Use regularly and they will thrive.

When the plant has finished flowering, chives should be cut down to a couple of inches high and, weather permitting, should start producing more leaves.

In the autumn, clumps can be divided if they are getting too big. Using a fork, dig around the plant and lift, being careful not to damage the roots. Separate the roots into two or more pieces and re-plant immediately.

Chive flowers can be eaten fresh and used as a garnish and can also be dried for winter use. The leaves won't dry well, but a few can be frozen if necessary. Freeze quickly on a tray, pack and label. Chives can normally be grown inside and outdoors all year round and storing is usually unnecessary.

Eating chives

Chives will add a mild onion flavour to all your favourite dishes. Cut into small pieces with kitchen scissors or chop finely with a sharp knife before using.

- Stir into a green salad or any mixed salad bowl.

- Make a potato salad. Steam or boil potatoes until tender. Drain well and cut into cubes, then leave to cool. Make a dressing of half mayonnaise and half natural yoghurt and add a handful of fresh chopped chives. When the potatoes are completely cold, stir in the dressing. Chill for 10 minutes before serving.

- Add chopped chives to beaten eggs before cooking an omelette or add to the pan after eggs have been cooking for a few minutes.

- Top cheese on toast with chopped chives and grill for a few seconds longer.

Chopped chives can be used as a garnish for many meals, from salads to meat and vegetable dishes.

CORIANDER

About coriander

Coriander is probably the most widely used herb round the world and is easy to grow. Fresh leaves add a distinct spicy flavour to any dish. Coriander seed is often added to sweet dishes.

Traditionally coriander was used to aid digestion and, although generally considered to be a culinary herb, it was used in many medicinal preparations throughout the centuries. Ancient Chinese cultures believed it to bestow immortality and seeds have been found in tombs over 5,000 years old.

Coriander growing

It is native to southern Europe and parts of Asia, and now grows wild in many parts of the world. It is an annual herb and should be planted every year, if the plants do not re-seed themselves.

Growing coriander

Coriander seed should be sown *in situ* as the seedlings don't transplant well. It likes a sunny spot but tends to run to seed quickly in too much sun. Grow some in partial shade and some in direct sun. The plants in the sunny spot will produce seed you can use in the kitchen or plant the following year. The plants in the semi-shady spot will produce more foliage and can be used fresh for many months.

Prepare the ground in early spring and rake to a fine tilth. Remove any perennial weeds and large stones. The seeds are large and easy to handle and should be placed about 1.5 in (4 cm) apart in shallow drills. Sow a short line every few weeks throughout spring and summer. Cover with a cloche at night if a frost is expected. When the seedlings are a few inches high, thin to allow about 8 in (20 cm) of growing room per plant. Pull out the weaker plants.

Coriander grows well in containers and indoors in pots. Make sure the soil in the pots doesn't dry out but is well drained.

Although coriander is an annual plant, it will often re-seed itself, and a coriander patch can keep going for many years. It will probably find its way around the garden but the plants aren't intrusive like mint – if they get in the way, simply pull them up and use in the kitchen.

Coriander has a strong scent and, like most herbs, will deter aphids and other pests. Plant some among your vegetable crops. It needs very little looking after once established.

Coriander leaves can be dried and stored for many months before they lose their flavour. Hang sprigs upside down in a dark airy place until dry and then crumble into jars and label. Store out of direct light.

Eating coriander

Coriander is a must-have herb for food lovers. It is an essential ingredient in curries and other spicy dishes.

- To make a simple chicken curry dish, cook chopped tomatoes with a chopped onion in a pan until the onion is soft. Add cooked chicken, cut into pieces (or use a vegetarian substitute). Mix in a handful of chopped fresh coriander and cook until the chicken is piping hot right through. Serve hot with rice or potatoes.

- Add fresh coriander leaves to a bread recipe with a little olive oil.

- Stir in some chopped fresh coriander before cooking homemade burgers or rissoles.

- Use a few feathery leaves as a garnish for any dish.

Experiment with coriander in the kitchen. As well as using the leaves, seed can be ground and used as a spice.

FENNEL

About fennel

Fennel can be grown for the leaves or as a vegetable crop. Fennel has been used in many medicinal preparations over the centuries and is believed to be a useful slimming aid. There seems to be hard evidence to support that as fennel does indeed aid digestion, although it also improves appetite.

Fennel growing and fennel bulb

Wild or home-cultivated seed is unlikely to produce a fennel bulb and hybrid seeds should be bought if you want to grow the vegetable rather than the herb. Fennel is a loner and prefers its own space in the garden.

Fennel is really a multi-purpose plant. The seed, leaves and bulbous root are all edible and very useful in the kitchen.

Growing fennel

Fennel is probably one of the easiest plants to grow in your herb garden, although cultivating the bulbous root requires a little more attention. The biggest problem you will probably face with growing fennel is its tendency to bolt in hot dry weather, and they can also bolt when transplanted. Water well and shade from the midday sun until they become established to avoid this.

Use biodegradable pots, if possible, to sow your seeds. This will help make the transplanting process smoother. Sow in early spring in fresh compost and keep pots warm and watered. The pots must be well drained. Plant out the seedlings in late spring to early summer. Check on your seed packet for variations.

Dig over the ground well before planting and remove any perennial weeds. Rake over the soil. Fennel isn't fond of heavy soil so add a little sharp sand if your soil is on the heavy side. Fennel inhibits the growth of dill, coriander and tomatoes and should be positioned as far away as possible from these plants.

Seed can be planted directly outside as long as there is no danger of frost. Cover with a cloche at night if the temperature drops too much. Fennel will also grow successfully in well-drained pots and containers, but shouldn't be allowed to dry out.

Each plant will need about 12 in (30 cm) of growing room. Allow about 2 ft (60 cm) between rows. Thinning will be necessary if you sow your seed directly outside in lines. Remove weaker plants.

Fennel deters white fly from your vegetable or herb bed but can be susceptible to caterpillars. Fennel can be left in the ground right through the autumn but won't survive a very heavy frost.

Use the leaves fresh. They can be dried or frozen but will lose some of their taste. Seed can be stored to add to pickles and relishes or saved to plant the following spring.

Eating fennel

Fennel has a very strong aniseed aroma and flavour. It is a well-known accompaniment to fish dishes.

- Fennel seeds can be used in pickles or crushed and added to soups, homemade burgers or sausages.

- Add flowers to herbal vinegars.

- Put a sprig of fresh fennel in a light oil, cover and leave for a few days before using.

- Chopped fresh fennel should be added to sauces and soups in the last minute or so of cooking time.

- Chop fresh fennel leaves and stir into a salad.

- Use the attractive feathery leaves as a garnish.

Cooking reduces the flavour so fennel should always be added to your recipe in the last minute or two of cooking unless otherwise advised in your recipe.

GARLIC

About garlic

Garlic has been cultivated for literally thousands of years and has all sorts of myths and legends attached to it, including keeping away vampires and bad spirits. Wild garlic has been around even longer. The Romans believed garlic brought strength and their soldiers were encouraged to include it in their daily diet.

Garlic is considered a useful food preservative, as well as being employed in medicinal preparations. It has effective anti-bacterial qualities and can help

Garlic growing and bulb

ward off colds and flu. Part of the onion family, garlic is strong in taste and scent and is also an easy herb to grow in the kitchen garden.

Growing garlic

Garlic is grown from cloves. It's best to buy a whole bulb from your garden centre to start. It can be grown from shop-bought cloves, but may not crop as well as a hybrid. If you do choose to propagate from a shop-bought bulb, buy an organic variety.

Cloves can be planted early in the spring. They are a hardy plant and will tolerate cold nights. Wait until the ground is workable and dig over, removing any perennial weeds. Rake to a fine tilth and remove any large stones. Plant garlic cloves in lines about 8 in (20 cm) apart, root end down. Leave the tip of the cloves just above the surface of the soil, but watch out for birds, as they can pull them out of the ground at this stage.

Keep weeds away and water if necessary. Because garlic is planted early in the year, it tends to get enough rainfall to grow well. Don't let garlic dry out in hot sun though.

Garlic has anti-bacterial properties that help protect it from disease and the strong odour deters pests. The only problem garlic has is that it can run to seed. If this happens, the plant will push up a flowering stem. Bend the stem down to the ground if this happens. Some growers pull these plants up as they don't store well. The cloves that have already developed can be used in the kitchen. These 'green' cloves will be stronger tasting.

Bulbs mature to full size anytime from July to September and should be harvested on a sunny day. Loosen the soil carefully around each one and pull up. Leave the plants lying on dry ground outside in the sun for a day. Store in single layers in boxes or plait and hang in a dark airy place for winter use.

Eating garlic

No good chef would be without garlic in the kitchen and a plait of garlic will encourage anyone to experiment with delicious recipes.

- Garlic bread is probably the most well known of the garlic recipes, and it's easy to make yourself. Cut slits in a French loaf, leaving about half an inch at the bottom of each cut to hold the loaf together. Blend butter with a couple of crushed garlic cloves, or more if you prefer, and some finely chopped fresh parsley. Using a knife, divide butter mixture between the slices, wrap in kitchen foil and place in a preheated medium oven for about 20 minutes or until hot right through. Serve hot.

- Add garlic to potato recipes. See garlic potatoes in chapter two.

- Chop or crush garlic cloves and add to bolognese and chilli dishes, as well as a little in the salad bowl to bring the tastes alive.

Every main meal recipe can be enhanced with a hint of garlic. Serve with fresh parsley to help freshen the breath.

MINT

About mint

Mint is a hardy perennial and will take over the garden if left to its own devices. Mint is probably one of the most well-known herbs in the UK, if only for its perfect accompaniment to roast lamb.

It is a known digestive aid and many people swear by mint tea after a meal. There are many different varieties, including spearmint, peppermint and penny royal. In recent years there have been a number of hybrids available, such as pineapple mint and, a very recent addition, chocolate mint that really does smell like chocolate mints!

Mint growing

Peppermint is probably the most practical variety to grow in the herb garden as it can be used in both sweet and savoury dishes.

Growing mint

Ideally mint should be contained as it can be a very invasive herb in the garden, and will take over a whole area in no time. Use large containers where possible or sink an old bottomless bucket into the ground, fill with soil and plant mint in that. The roots will eventually find their way out, but this does help to contain the plant a little.

Mint likes moisture, although it won't live in waterlogged soil. In full sun the soil will dry out too quickly for your plants, so this is an excellent herb to grow in a shady patch in the garden where other plants may not survive.

Propagate from seed or root division. Mint germinates well and is easy to grow from seed. Sow in well-drained trays of compost and transplant when the plants are large enough to handle, either into the garden or individual pots or containers. Water regularly.

To propagate from root division, simply break off a piece of the root of an established plant. Plant in compost and keep watered and weed free until the new plant starts growing and can be transplanted, if necessary.

Mint is a hardy plant and doesn't need much looking after once established, but it shouldn't be allowed to dry out. If your plants are in a sunny spot or there has been an unusually low rainfall, a mulch can help keep moisture in the roots.

Occasionally mint suffers from a 'rust' disease. The mint rust fungus enters the plant from the soil and permanently affects the whole plant. Signs are discolouration and often a kind of 'rash' on the underside of the leaves. Plants should be removed if this occurs and new plants placed in a different area.

Use leaves as soon as the plants start to grow, and pick off flowers to encourage more foliage. Mint can be dried successfully. Hang sprigs upside down in a dry dark airy place and crumble into jars and label. Store out of direct light.

Eating mint

Mint is a versatile herb and can be used as a digestive aid as well as a flavouring for many dishes. Peppermint and spearmint are the two most common varieties of mint used in the kitchen although there are many different types to try.

- Add fresh mint leaves in the last couple of minutes of cooking fresh peas, broad beans or new potatoes.

- Make a quick mint sauce by mixing finely chopped mint with vinegar. Leave to marinate for an hour before serving. Serve with roast lamb or any vegetable dish.

- Make tea! Pour boiling water on a sprig of mint in a jug and cover for five minutes. Stir and strain into a cup or glass.

- Experiment with mint in sweet dishes such as chocolate puddings or homemade ice cream.

OREGANO

About oregano

Oregano is sometimes known as wild marjoram. They belong to the same family but are in fact different herbs. Oregano grows wild in many parts of Europe and is a commercially viable product.

It is a low-growing shrub that stays green all year round in mild climates. It is also a nutritious herb full of vitamins and minerals and worthy of a place in your herb garden. It has been used in medicinal preparations for centuries and has antiseptic and sedative qualities. Oregano is an invaluable culinary herb, and can be grown in containers and pots as well as outside.

Oregano growing

Growing oregano

Oregano is a perennial herb and will come back every year, although plants are best replaced every three or four years as they can become straggly and 'woody'. Seeds germinate well and should be started quite early in the year. Put two or three seeds onto the surface of fresh compost in individual well-drained pots. Spray with water at least once or twice a day and keep in a warm place until the seedlings come up.

When the seedlings are large enough to handle, thin them to allow one seedling per pot. Plant out later when all danger of frost has passed. Oregano likes a sunny position and will be happy to grow in well-drained containers and hanging baskets as long as the compost doesn't dry out. Oregano is an ideal herb to grow on a patio or balcony.

Seeds can also be sown directly outside in late spring. Protect with a cloche at night until they are established and growing well. Thin plants to allow 12 in (30 cm) or more per plant, or transplant when they are large enough to handle.

The foliage is very brightly coloured, making oregano an attractive plant in the herb garden. Grow around your vegetables or as a border plant. It produces a warm humid atmosphere and is ideal to grow around a bed of sweet peppers.

Oregano is perfect for deterring aphids and black fly and plants can be placed around the vegetable garden to help keep your crops pest free.

Plants can be trimmed back and shaped, and should be used as much as possible. Start picking leaves when the plant is about 8 in (20 cm) tall. When flowers start to appear, pick off the flower heads to encourage the plant to produce more foliage.

Oregano is available fresh most of the year but can be dried for storing if needed. Hang sprigs upside down in a dark airy place. When completely dry, crumble into jars and label. Store out of direct light.

Eating oregano

Oregano is useful in many everyday dishes to add that extra zest to meat and vegetables. Here are a few ideas:

- Make a chopped green mixed salad. Add crumbled feta cheese and some chopped fresh oregano. Stir gently to mix and chill for 20 minutes before serving.

- Add fresh oregano to all tomato-based dishes such as bolognese.

- Oregano can be added to stir-fries and pasta dishes.

- Place a couple of sprigs of oregano over a chicken in the last 30 minutes or so of roasting.

Oregano is an attractive herb and is a perfect garnish for all meat or vegetable dishes.

PARSLEY

About parsley

Parsely is another well-known herb, but often underused. Parsley has nearly always been used as a garnish rather than added to dishes during cooking. It is however a very nutritious herb, containing significant amounts of iron and other minerals, as well as vitamins. Gram for gram, parsley has more vitamin C than citrus fruits.

There are a number of different varieties that can be used in the kitchen, including an Italian flat-leaved variety as well as the traditional curly leaf types.

Parsley growing

Parsley is very effective in freshening the breath and should always be added to meals containing garlic. It is a biennial plant, producing flowers and seed during the second year of growth before dying back.

Growing parsley

Parsley needs to be sown every year to ensure a fresh supply. During the second year of growth the plant puts its energy into producing flowers and seeds, so there won't be much foliage available for use.

Parsley likes rich soil and a sunny spot to thrive. It can be grown in containers or pots on a windowsill. Parsley will grow readily from seed but could take up to six weeks to germinate. Some growers soak seed in water before sowing to speed up the germination process.

Sow a few seeds in well-drained pots of fresh compost in the spring and keep warm and watered. When plants come up, remove the weaker ones to leave one plant per pot to grow on.

Seeds can be sown outside, but a little later in the year when all danger of frost has passed. Sow sparsely as plants will need thinning out to allow space to grow. Transplant parsley plants to a sunny spot in the garden. They will tolerate some shade but make sure the soil is rich to make up for the lack of sun. Parsley is a nutritious plant and draws its qualities from the soil. It will need an organic feed from time to time if your soil is of poor quality.

Start using leaves when the plants are about 8 in (20 cm) tall and keep using them right through the first year of growth. During the second year, allow the plants to produce flowers and seed. The seed can be collected and used in the kitchen or for sowing the following spring.

Whole stems of parsley can be frozen or dried. Lay sprigs on freezer trays and freeze quickly. Pack and label before storing. Hang sprigs up to dry in a dark airy place. Crumble into jars and label. Store out of direct light.

Eating parsley

Parsley is a perfect herb for garnishing but often gets left on the side of the plate. Chop finely and sprinkle over the dish to make it more palatable.

- Steam or boil any vegetables, drain well and toss in a little butter and finely chopped fresh parsley.

- Make a parsley soup. Melt 2 oz (50 g) of butter in a large saucepan. Add two stalks of celery, finely sliced, and one chopped onion. Cook gently until the vegetables are starting to change colour. Stir in 1 tbsp of flour and slowly add 1.5 pt (900 ml) of vegetable or chicken stock. Add 4 oz (100 g) of chopped fresh parsley and a little seasoning. Bring to the boil, then reduce heat and simmer for about 20 minutes. Allow to cool, then blend in a liquidiser or blender until smooth. Return to the heat and cook gently until hot right through, stirring to prevent burning.

- Scrub parsley root, slice and add to stews and casseroles.

Parsley should be used as much as possible in the kitchen, not only for its taste but also for its wonderful nutritional qualities.

ROSEMARY

About rosemary

Rosemary has many myths and legends attached to it. At various times throughout history it has been used to ward off evil spirits, and used in ceremonies such as weddings and baptisms. It has often been employed in medicinal preparations to soothe colds, headaches and digestive problems.

Rosemary is a hardy perennial and once established in the herb garden, can last for 20 years before it needs to be replaced. It has been cultivated in herb gardens for many centuries.

More often used in cooking these days than as a medicinal herb, rosemary is invaluable in the kitchen.

Rosemary growing

Growing rosemary

Rosemary is notoriously difficult to propagate from seed. Germination is poor and can take up to three months. It is possible though, and seed should be sown in well-drained trays of fresh compost in the spring and kept warm until seedlings are ready to plant out. Check on the seed packets for manufacturer's growing recommendations before you start.

The most effective way to start off rosemary is by taking a cutting from an established plant. Although you will probably only need one or two rosemary plants in the herb garden, start off a number of cuttings in case some don't work.

Take 3–4 in (8–10 cm) cuttings just above or below a leaf joint from a healthy plant. Use a sharp knife or secateurs to avoid damage to the stem. Push cuttings, cut end down, into well-drained pots of fresh compost then water. Keep plants warm and don't allow the compost to dry out.

Cuttings should produce roots in three or four months, when they will be ready to transplant into the garden. Rosemary is suitable for container growing, although shrubs can grow quite big so plants may need re-potting after a year or so.

When you plant them in the garden, choose a well-drained sunny spot and allow 2 or 3 ft (60–90 cm) all round for the plant to grow. Water well after planting.

Rosemary is a hardy plant and will tolerate very cold weather, and often stay fresh and usable right through the winter months. The plant has also been known to survive near drought conditions, although watering fairly regularly in hot dry periods will ensure it grows well.

Although rosemary is evergreen and should be available all year round, it can be dried and stored by hanging sprigs until dry and stripping leaves off into a jar. Store out of direct light.

Eating rosemary

Rosemary is traditionally cooked with pork, fish and chicken although it is also often used with roast lamb or lamb chops.

- Rosemary isn't often used in salads, but can be added to salad dressings, oils and vinegars. Place a sprig in a bottle of white wine vinegar or a light cooking oil. Seal and leave for a couple of weeks before using.

- Throw a few fresh sprigs on the coals of a barbeque. Also, leaves can be stripped and the stalks used as skewers.

- Chop leaves finely or crumble dried rosemary leaves onto pizzas, in pasta dishes and tomato sauces.

Rosemary imparts a wonderful pine aroma when burned or bruised and has a very distinctive taste.

SAGE

About sage

Sage is a hardy perennial but should be replaced every four or five years before it gets too woody. Ancient people believed it to be a herb of wisdom, hence the common name. It was grown to help drown bad smells in medieval times and the Romans believed it to be a herb of immortality.

It has been used in many medicinal preparations to treat fevers, stomach problems and even memory loss. In recent years research has proven sage to be helpful in alleviating menopausal symptoms such as hot flushes.

Sage growing

It has been cultivated as a medicinal and culinary herb for thousands of years. Originating in Mediterranean areas, sage is now widely grown and many varieties are available including attractive variegated types.

Growing sage

A lot of patience is needed if you want to grow sage from seed as it will be over a year before it is usable. Small plants can be bought from garden centres and larger supermarkets. Otherwise, get your sage plants going by cuttings or layering. There are many attractive varieties available, and they can be used as border plants for the herb or vegetable garden.

Sage is a woody plant and will develop roots from the stems quite readily. From a well-established plant, layer a healthy bottom branch down to the ground and hold in place with a V-shaped peg. Water and keep free of weeds until roots develop. Then the plant can be transplanted if necessary.

Sage can also be propagated from cuttings from a well-established plant. In the spring or summer, take 3–4 in (8–10 cm) cuttings from healthy branches and push into potting compost in well-drained containers. Keep pots warm until they start growing well, and then transplant into the garden or larger pots and containers.

Sage doesn't need a lot of maintaining or watering. Later in the year, the plants become straggly but can be cut back to the shape you want them.

Sage will thrive in well-drained soil and will do well in rock gardens or raised beds. They don't like very long cold spells, so are best planted in containers that can be moved to a warmer environment if you have cold winters. In moderate climates sage will be available all year round outside.

Sage flowers can be candied and leaves can be dried. Dry sprigs in a dark airy place, crumble into jars and label. Store out of direct light to help retain the flavour. The leaves can also be frozen.

Eating sage

Sage isn't a cure-all but does have important healing properties and a glass of sage tea every day will give the system a boost.

- Sage and onion stuffing is probably the most well-known sage recipe. Peel four onions and leave whole. Add to saucepan of water and bring to the boil. Reduce the heat and simmer for about 10 minutes. During the last couple of minutes, add ten sage leaves. Drain and chop finely in a large mixing bowl. Add 5 oz (125 g) of breadcrumbs, 1.5 oz (40 g) of unsalted softened butter and seasoning to taste. Bind with the yolk of an egg and shape into balls to bake or use to stuff a turkey or chicken.

- Add a chopped leaf or two to rissoles, burgers or vegetable croquettes.

- Mix with other herbs, such as basil and thyme, and use in stews and casseroles.

Sage is a very strong tasting herb and should be used sparingly. Too much can make food taste bitter.

THYME

About thyme

Thyme has played a part in everyday family life for many centuries and has many myths and legends surrounding it. Once it was believed that if a woman wore a sprig of thyme behind her ear she would attract a husband. Nowadays we tend to just throw it in the pot and cook a nice meal!

Thyme is used in many medicinal preparations to help alleviate cold and flu symptoms, and is very effective. It has been cultivated for medicinal and culinary use for hundreds of years and is considered to be a good preservative for meat.

Thyme is a hardy perennial and will grace your herb garden for many years. It originates from Mediterranean areas and will tolerate very dry conditions. Thyme has an unmistakeable sweet smell and is a good herb to grow in containers on a patio where the leaves are brushed against to release the scent.

Thyme growing

Growing thyme

Growing thyme from seed is very satisfying but it will be a while before you can use it. Seed can be sown early in the year in well-drained trays or pots of compost and kept inside or in a greenhouse until the plants are large enough to handle, and all danger of frost has passed.

The seed can also be sown outside from around May onwards. Sow thinly as the plants will need space when they come up. Thin seedlings to allow around 2 ft (60 cm) of space for each plant. Don't use any leaves in the first year though.

Thyme can also be propagated from cuttings or root division. To start from cuttings, take 3–4 inch (8–10 cm) cuttings from a healthy established plant and push them, cut side down, into pots of fresh compost. Make sure the pots are well drained. Keep in a warm sunny spot or indoors until the plants start to grow. In the following spring, cuttings that have developed roots can be transplanted.

Every three or four years, thyme becomes straggly and should be divided. Dig the whole plant up carefully to avoid damaging the roots. Pull the roots apart and re-plant the healthiest pieces into pots or containers, or directly into the herb garden.

Position thyme in a sunny spot and water occasionally but never allow it to become too wet. In very cold winters, mulch to protect the roots from freezing.

Thyme is best eaten fresh and will stay green practically all year round, especially if you keep a pot going on a windowsill indoors. It can be dried by hanging stems upside down in a dark airy place then storing in a sealed jar. Label and keep out of direct light. Whole stems can be frozen. Pick before flowers appear and freeze quickly.

Eating thyme

Thyme is slow to release its flavour and should be added early in the cooking time.

- Put a couple of whole fresh sprigs in the roasting tin when cooking a joint of lamb or a chicken.

- The tiny thyme leaves can be mixed into burger and rissole mixtures before cooking.

- Sprinkle a few in the salad bowl or use as a garnish for green salads and cold tomato dishes.

- Make tea. Steep a sprig of thyme in freshly boiled water for five minutes and strain into a cup or glass.

- Add to casseroles, soups and stews, and include a sprig of thyme when bunching together herbs for a *bouquet garni* mix.

Thyme is a useful herb to have in the kitchen and enhances the taste of fish and chicken as well as vegetarian dishes.

CHAPTER 5
FRUITY TREATS

Apples and pears have been grown in British gardens for many years, but traditionally in the form of huge trees that overshadowed the rest of the garden. There are practical hybrid varieties available now that will stay fairly small in the home garden. Many apple and pear trees will be grafted although this can be done at home. A certain amount of expertise is required to get it right. Dwarf apple and pear trees can be grown very successfully in a small space and it is worth browsing the varieties available in your local garden centre to decide which ones are best for you.

This chapter concentrates on growing soft fruits as well as lemons. Although lemons originate from Mediterranean areas, oranges and lemons have been grown in hothouses for many years in the UK. The Victorians prided themselves on their orangeries where they grew oranges, lemons and limes. These were, however, mostly connected to wealthy houses as it took an army of gardeners to produce the fruits.

Lemon trees have become very popular over the last few years right across Europe. New hybrid varieties will produce lemons without having to be kept in hothouses, although a certain amount of care is needed to produce a good crop.

This chapter covers five everyday fruits:

- strawberries

- blackberries

- blackcurrants

- raspberries

- lemons.

All of these fruits will grow happily outdoors in the UK climate, although lemons are best grown in containers so that they may be brought indoors during the winter months.

Blackberries grow wild in many parts and can be collected and eaten, although they shouldn't be collected from certain areas (see page 120). New thorn-less varieties are available that are not quite as hardy as the original bramble but are more practical in a home garden.

Strawberries, raspberries and blackcurrants have been favourite garden fruits for many generations and you don't need a Ph.D. in botany to grow them. But they will get you lots of brownie points!

STRAWBERRIES

About strawberries
Wild strawberries have been around for thousands of years over many parts of the world. The cultivated strawberry is much sweeter and wild strawberries

are rarely collected these days, although they are useful for cooking. Cultivated strawberries first came to the home garden around the sixteenth century and symbolised sweetness and purity. It was once believed that if two sweethearts each ate half of a heart-shaped strawberry, they would fall deeply in love.

Strawberries are easy to grow at home and can be grown in special strawberry planters or any other suitable container, as well as directly outside. There are varieties that will crop more than once a year.

Properties of strawberries

Strawberries are rich in vitamins, in particular vitamin C, and have long been used as a healing herb as well as a special treat in cakes and desserts. They also contain dietary fibre. Strawberry leaf tea is available in health food shops and is a well-established healthy addition to the diet.

Strawberries have been said to cure many ailments including kidney conditions and throat infections. They contain phenol which is an anti-inflammatory and they have been found to be an effective treatment for asthma and rheumatoid arthritis.

Growing strawberries

There are many different varieties of strawberry, including seasonal varieties, which means that with a little careful planning you will be able to grow a couple of different varieties and be harvesting fruit for a long period throughout the year.

Choose a type that produces lots of smaller fruits if you have children. The larger ones will take longer to grow and ripen and, as kids love to pick and eat strawberries, you may as well grow as many as you can.

Don't attempt to start your strawberry bed from wild plants. They are unlikely to produce sweet fruits and will stay very small. The best way to start is to beg some spare plants from a local grower. Every year strawberries put out runners and produce new plants, so there may be some available from a neighbouring gardener. Alternatively, local garden centres usually have a good choice of healthy plants.

A strawberry bed should be moved ideally every few years but you need to find a semi-permanent patch in full sun to get them going. They shouldn't be planted in the same soil that has grown tomatoes, potatoes or peppers in the previous few years. These vegetables can leave a virus in the ground that can damage strawberry plants.

In the autumn before spring plantings dig over the ground and incorporate plenty of well-rotted manure or compost. Remove any perennial weeds and non-organic debris. In the following spring, the ground will need just a light dig and raking over. Strawberry plants grow rather straggly and it's a good idea to place bricks or wood around the bed to keep the plants contained and also to help with maintenance. Don't make the bed too wide. You want to be able to reach the middle from both sides.

Plant strawberry plants so that the roots are covered but not the 'crown'. Allow around 12 in (30 cm) between plants and 18 in (45 cm) between rows. This is a general guide. Check on any special variations when you buy your plants. Water them well after planting.

Although strawberries are a popular fruit to grow at home, there are conflicting ideas about caring for them. Some growers believe you should pick off all the flowers in the first year so that the plants become established and produce strong root growth. The best way is to go with your instincts and advice from growers in your area.

Generally, strawberry plants must be watered regularly and kept weed free. In the hot sun, the soil can dry out quickly so a mulch is useful during the summer

Strawberry plants

months. A mulch of straw will help deter slugs as well. As soon as the fruits appear they are vulnerable to slug and bird attacks. The straw will help deter the slugs but bird-friendly netting may be necessary to stop the birds eating all your fruit.

Strawberry plants can be damaged by extreme cold and should be protected during the winter with a cloche or other protection.

The 'mother' plants will send off runners during the growing season. These can be cut from the plant in autumn and re-planted to extend your strawberry bed, or to start a new one. These new baby plants will root themselves if they can and may be left if you wish but the bed will get untidy. Also fruits need space to develop so don't let the strawberry bed become too overcrowded.

Pick strawberries as soon as they are ripe. Don't leave them to rot on the plants.

Eating strawberries

Strawberries are best eaten fresh straight off the plant, or chilled for ten minutes or so in the fridge. Top with double or whipped cream and garnish with a mint leaf or two for an elegant Sunday afternoon tea!

STRAWBERRY JAM

If your strawberry bed takes off and you have more fruit than you know what to do with, make strawberry jam. A couple of jars of homemade jam brings the family a wonderful taste of summer in the winter months.

This recipe will make about 5 lb of jam. Prepare jars in advance by washing and drying in a low oven to sterilise. Then prepare the fruit. Remove any leaves and stalks from 3 lb (1.4 kg) of strawberries and halve them. Rinse under slow running water and drain well.

Place the strawberries in a large heavy-based pan with the juice of half a lemon. Bring to the boil over a medium heat then reduce the heat and simmer for 20–30 minutes until the fruit is soft. Stir regularly to prevent sticking. Remove from the heat and stir in 3 lb (1.4 kg) of sugar, stirring until the sugar has dissolved.

Return to the heat and boil rapidly for about 20 minutes. Test for a setting point, using a sugar thermometer if you have one. The temperature needs to be 221°F (105°C). If you don't have a sugar thermometer, test for a set by dropping a small teaspoonful of jam onto a cold saucer. Rub the surface of the jam after a few seconds. If it wrinkles, then it's ready.

Pour carefully into warm jars, seal and label. Store out of direct light.

OTHER STRAWBERRY IDEAS
- Use to decorate and fill Victoria sponge cakes. Cut strawberries in half and lay on the cream or jam filling, then place the other layer of cake on top. After dusting with icing sugar, arrange a few halved strawberries and mint leaves on top.

- Add a few to muesli or any other breakfast cereal. A few strawberries in the morning is a healthy way to start your 5-a-day fruit and veg. Use a juicer or blender and add a couple of strawberries to a banana smoothie or a milkshake.

- Mix a few strawberries, cut in half or quarters, into a fruit salad or top your favourite dessert with some.

- Make a strawberry pie or crumble. Lay halved strawberries in an ovenproof dish and top with a pastry crust or crumble mix. A simple crumble mix can be made by rubbing 2 oz (50 g) of hard butter or margarine, cut into small pieces, into 4 oz (100 g) of flour, until the mixture resembles breadcrumbs. Add a little more flour if the mix becomes sticky. Stir in 2 oz (50 g) of sugar and spread over the top of the fruit. Bake in the oven (Gas Mark 4, 350°F, 180°C) for about half an hour or until the crumble is starting to go brown. Don't overcook or it will be too dry. Serve hot with custard or cream.

BLACKBERRIES

About blackberries

Blackberry plants, or brambles as they are commonly known, have been growing wild over many parts of Europe for hundreds if not thousands of years. With the reduction in hedgerows and the fact that there is generally less countryside to go around, the bramble is now often grown as a hybrid in the home garden.

Wild blackberries can be collected, but care should be taken. Don't collect blackberries from the side of the road as they can absorb car pollution. They are also susceptible to chemical sprays and therefore shouldn't be collected from areas near to farmland unless the farm is definitely organic. Also, dogs can pollute low growing fruit. But even taking all those factors into account, there are many from the wild that can still be harvested.

The hybrids available for home growing are less hardy than the original hardy bramble, but they take up less space and as a bonus many of them are thorn-less.

Properties of blackberries

Blackberry fruits and leaves have a high vitamin and mineral content. The fruits are high in vitamin C and the leaves have been used as a medicinal aid for many years. They effectively alleviate symptoms of diarrhoea and other stomach problems. They are also said to help soothe mouth ulcers. Blackberry is a good tonic and a cup of blackberry leaf tea every day will help boost the immune system and prevent colds and flu bugs.

The fruits and leaves also contain anti-oxidants which help fight against free radicals therefore preventing some cancers and heart disease.

Growing blackberries

Anyone who has ever taken over a neglected garden or piece of land will know that brambles aren't to be messed with! If you're facing a bramble patch that needs to be sorted, it's tempting to plough the whole lot up – or preferably dynamite it. However, brambles are very hardy plants and if you have a few that could be left and trained to grow where you want them, it's a good idea to tackle them by hand. Arm yourself with a strong pair of shears and protective clothing before you start.

Blackberries

For most of us wanting to grow a few blackberries in the garden, a wild bramble patch isn't an option. Blackberry plants can be grown from seed but will take a long time of looking after before they germinate. The best way to propagate a blackberry patch is either to buy hybrids from a local garden supplier or start your plants using cuttings or by the layering method.

Take cuttings from a healthy plant after the fruit has finished in the autumn. Push cuttings into compost in a seed bed, pots or containers and keep an eye on them until the following spring when it should have developed roots. They will then be ready to plant out in their final position. Blackberries are one of the few fruits that will mature in the shade, so if all the sunny spots are taken blackberries can fill a shady spot in your garden.

If the plants have some sun though, they will develop larger fruits and they may be slightly sweeter. Choose your spot carefully if you are planting hybrids. These should come with growing recommendations when you buy them. The area must be well drained. Never plant blackberry canes in waterlogged soil. The soil should be kept moist, so water regularly if they are getting a lot of sun.

Brambles can also be layered. As with many plants with woody stems, blackberries will produce roots from the stem. Choose a healthy lower branch from a well-established plant and peg to the ground with a V-shaped peg where it naturally touches the soil. Water regularly. Mulch during cold weather and by the following spring it should be developing roots.

When new cuttings or layered plants have developed roots, they can be planted out. However, if a long hot summer is expected it may be better to leave them until the following autumn. Keep them watered.

Allow about 18 in (45 cm) between plants when you plant your new canes out. Generally plants started from a hardy rootstock won't need much watering or any other attention, but hybrid varieties may need a little extra care.

Harvest fruits when they are fully black and fall off the stem at a touch. They will keep for a few days in the fridge, but are better eaten on the same day as picking. After fruits have finished, plants can be pruned and new cuttings taken. Most blackberry types will survive very low temperatures but if you are concerned for your variety of blackberry mulch with grass cuttings or straw over the winter, remembering to remove any un-rotted material early in the spring to aerate the soil.

Eating blackberries

Collecting blackberries with the kids always has an air of anticipation about it. If you can persuade them not to eat too many while they are picking, they will look forward to a blackberry and apple crumble without a doubt.

BLACKBERRY AND APPLE CRUMBLE

Peel and slice a couple of cooking apples and put them into a pan with a little water. Bring gently to the boil then reduce the heat and simmer until the apples are starting to soften. You could use dessert apples, which will take less time to soften. Very soft apples may need no cooking at all.

When the apples are prepared put them into an ovenproof dish with as many washed and cleaned blackberries as you can find or will fit. Sprinkle a little sugar over the fruit and add a couple of tablespoons of water.

Top with a crumble mixture (see strawberry crumble recipe, page 120) and cook in a preheated oven (Gas Mark 4, 350°F, 180°C) for about half an hour or until the crumble topping starts to go brown. Don't cook it for too long as the crumble will become dry. Serve hot with custard or cold with cream.

INDIVIDUAL BLACKBERRY PIES AND TARTS

Blackberries are a very soft fruit and need little cooking so are ideal for making 'jam' tarts. Line patty tins with pastry and fill with mashed blackberries instead of jam. Sprinkle a little sugar over the fruit and bake for about 10–15 minutes in a preheated oven (Gas Mark 5, 375°F, 190°C) or until the pastry is cooked.

To make individual pies, line the patty tins with pastry and bake 'blind' for 5 or 10 minutes until the pastry is set. (To bake blind, place a circle of greaseproof paper on each pastry case and put a few dried beans on top. Remove the paper and beans after removing from the oven.) Spoon mashed blackberries into the pastry cases and cover with a circle of pastry. Brush with beaten egg or milk to glaze. Cook as before until the pastry is golden brown. Remove from the oven and sprinkle a small amount of sugar over each pie while they are still hot. Serve hot or cold.

BLACKBERRY AND APPLE JAM
This is yet another delicious recipe using blackberries and apples together. This recipe will make about 5 lb (2.25 kg) of jam. Prepare the jars and keep warm. Remove all leaves and stems and gently rinse 2 lb (0.9 kg) of blackberries. Put them in a large saucepan with about 75 ml of water. Bring gently to the boil, then reduce the heat and simmer until the fruit is soft.

Peel, core and slice 12 oz (350 g) of cooking apples and put them in a large heavy-based pan with 75 ml of water. Simmer gently until the apples are soft. Mash the apples with a potato masher or wooden spoon then add the blackberries to the apple pulp. Immediately stir in 3 lb (1.4 kg) of sugar and keep stirring until the sugar has dissolved.

Bring to the boil and keep boiling for about 10 minutes, stirring often. Test for a setting point with a thermometer or by putting a small spoonful of jam onto a cold saucer. If after a few seconds the jam forms a skin, the setting point has been reached. Remove from the heat and pour into warm jars. Never pour hot jam into cold jars as the glass will break. Label and store out of direct light.

OTHER BLACKBERRY IDEAS

Blackberries can also be added to:

- fruit salads

- ice cream desserts

- yoghurts

- smoothies.

Blackberries are a popular ingredient in wine making and are often used with grapes or on their own to produce a country wine.

BLACKCURRANTS

About blackcurrants

Blackcurrants must be one of the world's most commercially grown crops. Blackcurrant juice has become a favourite cordial for children and adults, and blackcurrants are also widely used in alcoholic beverages.

Blackcurrants have been picked in the wild for probably thousands of years and used in medicinal preparations since the Middle Ages. It wasn't until the nineteenth and twentieth centuries that research uncovered just how power packed this simple little fruit is. With high quantities of vitamin C it is probably one of the best garden fruits to grow. Bushes take up relatively little space and are hardy perennials, making them a good crop to grow in less than warm climates.

Properties of blackcurrants

During the Second World War vitamin C was hard to come by and, when it was discovered that blackcurrants are one of the highest sources of vitamin C, farmers and households alike were encouraged to grow them. Practically the whole farmed crop of blackcurrants at that time was used to make cordials and British children have been drinking it ever since.

Blackcurrants are also a good source of calcium, iron and protein.

Blackcurrants are still a highly valued commercial crop and they are also quite straightforward to grow in a home garden.

Growing blackcurrants

Blackcurrants are propagated from canes (cuttings) from established and healthy plants. They like a sunny position but will tolerate some shade if necessary.

Although the blackcurrant plant is a hardy perennial, and will cope with most soil types, the ground must be well drained. It's a good idea to do a little preparation before planting. Dig over the area and remove any perennial weeds, non-organic debris and large stones, and dig in some well-rotted manure or compost during the autumn before spring plantings.

Hybrid plants are normally available during the winter to early spring from garden suppliers. Choose a variety that requires little maintenance or, alternatively, start your blackcurrants from cuttings.

After harvesting all fruits, take cuttings from a well-established plant and push into a bed or large container of fresh compost. Keep watered but don't allow the soil to become waterlogged. The cuttings should develop roots over the following year and be ready to plant out in the following autumn, or before.

As long as the ground is workable and not too wet or frozen, plant out shop-bought or home produced plants in the garden anytime from autumn to

Blackcurrants

spring. Each plant needs about 6 ft (2 m) of growing room and should be positioned in a sunny spot if possible.

Water plants well and don't allow them to dry out. To keep moisture in the ground, you can apply a mulch. Mulch helps to keep weeds away and moisture in. Use a good quality garden compost as a mulch and you will also be feeding the soil at the same time.

Harvest blackcurrants when they are ready. Don't leave them on the bush for the birds or, worse, let them rot. They should be picked on a dry day where possible, wet blackcurrants will perish much faster than dry picked ones. If you pick them when they are dry they can be stored in the fridge for a couple of days.

Leave the plants to grow in their first year but prune back in subsequent years after harvesting all the fruits. You may have specific pruning recommendations for your variety of blackcurrant but, generally, use a sharp pair of secateurs and cut away about 20% of the wood from the middle of the plant and a little from the outside, but not too much. Tidy each plant up by cutting out crossed branches. Prune carefully and the plant will last for many years and produce more blackcurrants every season.

Blackcurrants aren't suitable for container growing. They don't thrive if their root growth is restricted. They are also better grown outside unless you are in a particularly hard growing region. Possibly near to the coast they will need some protection from the wind. Otherwise blackcurrants are a hardy bush and will last for many years in a home garden.

Eating blackcurrants

As well as the infamous juices and other drinks, blackcurrants can be used in many recipes.

BLACKCURRANT JAM

Prepare enough jars to hold around 10 lb (4.5 kg) of jam. Wash and dry in a very low oven with the door ajar until ready to use.

Prepare 4 lb (1.8 kg) of blackcurrants. Remove stalks, leaves and any damaged fruit and wash under running water and drain. Put the fruit into a heavy-based, or preserving, pan with 3 pt (1.7 l) of water. Bring to the boil, then reduce the heat and simmer for about 45 minutes, stirring often to prevent the fruit sticking to the pan.

When the fruit is tender and the contents of the pan have been reduced, remove from the heat and stir in 6 lb (2.7 kg) of sugar. Stir until the sugar has dissolved, then return to the heat and boil rapidly for about 10 minutes. Test for a set (see the blackberry and apple jam recipe in the previous section, page 124) then pour into warm jars and label. Store out of direct light.

BLACKCURRANT TART

Preheat the oven to Gas Mark 6, 400°F, 200°C. Prepare and wash 1 lb (450 g) of blackcurrants. Pour a little water in an ovenproof dish (to prevent fruit from sticking) and pour in about half the blackcurrants. Sprinkle with 3 oz (75 g) of sugar and put the rest of the fruit on top. Cover with a pastry crust and glaze with milk or beaten egg. Bake in the preheated oven for about 45 minutes. The top of the dish can be loosely covered with silver foil to prevent over-browning.

To make a pastry crust, cut 2 oz (50 g) of butter or margarine into small cubes and rub into 4 oz (100 g) of flour with your fingertips, until the mixture resembles fine breadcrumbs. Add a little more flour if the mixture is too sticky. Add water, a little at a time, and press the mixture together until it forms a dough. Knead gently and then roll out on a floured board. Cut the pastry to the required size and cover the fruit with it.

MORE BLACKCURRANT IDEAS

- Make your own blackcurrant juice. Clean the fruit, add water and bring to the boil. Reduce the heat and simmer until the fruit is soft. Allow to cool and blend in a food processor or liquidiser, adding more water if a more diluted juice is required. Add a little lemon juice or honey according to taste or simply leave it natural. Sugar can be added if blackcurrants aren't sweet enough. Pour into a sterilised bottle to store for a few days.

- Make your own juice then freeze it in ice-lolly moulds – fresh organic blackcurrant ice lollies!

- Cook blackcurrants and mash or blend, then mix with ice cream or cream to make a quick and delicious dessert. Sprinkle with a little sugar if blackcurrants are a little tart in taste.

- Add a few to fruit salads.

Blackcurrants can be kept for a few days in the fridge, as long as they are dry when picked and unwashed before storing. It is possible to freeze them, but some texture and taste will be lost. They are better used in recipes before freezing.

RASPBERRIES

About raspberries

It is believed that raspberries have been available across many parts of the world since prehistoric times. It wasn't until the sixteenth century that they were cultivated and different strains were recorded from the eighteenth century.

There are many different varieties of raspberry that can be grown in the home garden. The plants take up little space and can be grown as a border. Your local garden supplier should have different varieties available, including golden and purple raspberries.

Raspberries have always been considered to be a healthy food and are a good source of vitamins. Because they are a soft fruit and don't travel well, they are often expensive to buy, which makes them even more attractive to grow at home.

Properties of raspberries

Raspberries are a good source of dietary fibre, having 6.5 g of fibre per 100 g, as well as being rich in vitamins and minerals. They contain around 50% more antioxidants than strawberries and help fight against cell damaging diseases.

Raspberries have a high vitamin C content as well as a significant amount of vitamin E, not always found in fruits and vegetables. They lose about half their vitamin C content in freezing, so should be eaten fresh wherever possible.

Growing raspberries

Before you buy raspberry canes, browse through a catalogue or two as there are many new and interesting varieties available from most garden suppliers.

Buy healthy canes that have well-developed roots or start off your own plants from cuttings. Take cuttings from a well-established plant after all the fruit has been harvested and push the cuttings, cut end down, into a large pot or seedbed of fresh compost. Keep weed free and watered until the following autumn, when roots should have developed. Start as many cuttings as you can because not all of them may be successful.

Raspberries, like most soft fruits, prefer a sunny spot in the garden. They are a hardy plant and will produce fruit in a partially shady spot but the fruits may not develop as well as those growing in full sun.

Prepare the ground by digging over and removing any perennial weeds and non-organic debris. Make sure the soil is well drained. Incorporate some sand or very light gravel to help with drainage if necessary. Plant your canes or rooted cuttings in the autumn to winter months. Raspberry canes can be planted in the spring as well, but are unlikely to produce much fruit during the first year.

Dig a trench for the canes and plant them about 12–18 in (30–45 cm) apart along the row and leave about 2–3 ft (60–90 cm) between rows. Some types of raspberry will benefit from a support system. Check on the growing recommendations before you plant for variations on distance and any advice on supporting the plants.

Plant canes in the trench and fill with fresh rich compost. Heel the canes in firmly and water well. If a very cold winter is expected, it is advisable to mulch around the new canes for the first year to prevent damage to the new roots.

With a sharp pair of secateurs, cut canes down to about 10–12 in (25–30 cm) straight after planting to encourage growth. In the following spring after planting, new suckers may appear which can be removed and re-planted. The new suckers should be transplanted every year to avoid overcrowding.

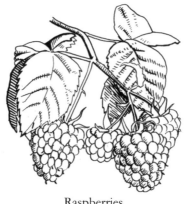

Raspberries

Mulch during the spring with organic material. In the summer, cut the original cane down to the ground and let the new branches produce the fruit. Raspberries fruit on new wood every year. After harvesting, the old wood should be removed, new suckers transplanted and then the remaining canes should be mulched for the winter months. Raspberries are heavy feeders and will benefit from a good organic feed from time to time.

Most raspberries are hardy and won't need any other protection in the cold weather. Check on your particular variety before planting but generally they don't need valuable polytunnel or indoor space. They are not particularly suitable for container growing as the roots need a large area to spread, and some varieties grow tall and will need support that isn't always practical within a container.

Don't let your raspberry canes dry out but make sure the area is well drained.

Eating raspberries

Raspberries are best eaten fresh on the day you pick them, but will keep for a couple of days in the fridge. They can be frozen but will lose some of the texture and taste. Freeze quickly if you want to keep some for the winter.

Raspberries are very soft and can be easily mashed to a puree and mixed with rice puddings, ice cream or made into fruit tartlets. To make individual tartlets, see the above recipe for blackberry pies and tarts and replace blackberries with raspberries.

RASPBERRY MERINGUE

This is an extra special Sunday treat! Preheat the oven to Gas Mark ¼, 225°F or 110°C. Cut an 8 in (20 cm) circle of greaseproof paper and place on a baking tin. Whisk three egg whites until very stiff then gradually add 3 oz (75 g) of sugar a little at a time. Whisk well after each addition. Then fold in another 3 oz (75 g) of sugar gently with a metal spoon.

Spread some of the meringue mixture over the greaseproof paper. Then make a thick rim around the circle with the rest of the meringue to form a case. Bake in the oven for 2½ to 3 hours. If the meringue starts going brown, leave the oven door ajar for the rest of the cooking time.

Remove from the oven and allow to cool completely. When cold, fill the meringue case with prepared raspberries – around 12 oz (375 g) should be enough. Then whip 10 fl oz (300 ml) of whipping cream and pipe or pile on top of the raspberries. Serve immediately.

RASPBERRY JAM

If you have more raspberries than you can eat, a pot or two of homemade raspberry jam is a wonderful store cupboard ingredient.

This recipe makes about 6.5 lb (3 kg) of jam. Prepare jars in advance by washing thoroughly and drying in a slow oven to sterilise. Prepare 4 lb (1.8 kg) of raspberries by removing any leaves and damaged fruit, then rinse and drain.

Put the raspberries in a large heavy-based saucepan or preserving pan. Bring to the boil, then lower the heat and simmer for about 20 minutes, stirring from time to time to prevent sticking. After 20 minutes, or when the fruit is soft, remove from the heat and stir in 4 lb (1.8 kg) of sugar. Stir until sugar has dissolved.

Return to the heat and boil rapidly for about 30 minutes. Test for a setting point as in the strawberry jam recipe (see page 119). When setting point is reached, remove from the heat and leave to stand for 15 minutes. Spoon into warm clean jars. Make sure the jars are warm or they may crack when pouring in hot jam.

MORE RASPBERRY IDEAS

- Add a few raspberries to breakfast cereals or yoghurts.

- Stir raspberries gently into a fruit salad.

- Make smoothies and mix with other berries or bananas.

- Puree raspberries to mix into ice cream or any other favourite dessert.

LEMONS

About lemons

Lemons, along with other citrus fruits such as oranges and limes, are indigenous to warmer climates. In Victorian times in England, the rich grew their own citrus fruits in large orangeries staffed by an army of gardeners. The individual fruits worked out to be very expensive.

In recent years, lemons have become a popular shrub in many parts of the world and although they need a little attention new hybrid varieties make it a lot easier to harvest your own lemons, even if you don't live in the Mediterranean.

There are a number of different lemons you can grow, and they are worth their weight in gold, especially when it comes to adding a slice to your favourite drink!

Properties of lemons

One peeled lemon weighing approximately 58 grams contains around 30 mg of vitamin C. Lemons are low in calories and also are a source of dietary fibre. They are used in many medicinal preparations, and have been for generations. The most well known is probably lemon and honey which is a perfect combination for soothing symptoms of colds and flu.

Lemons are also employed in cleaning products because of their grease-cutting properties. Lemon juice will dry the skin if in contact for any length of time. Lemon juice has also been used as a bleaching agent for hair colouring and at one time was thought to remove freckles if dabbed on gently. However, there is little scientific evidence to support this as being a healthy cosmetic exercise, particularly as lemon juice will dry the skin.

Growing lemons

Lemons need a warm sunny spot and won't survive temperatures of less than $-1°C$ or $30°F$. Always protect against cold weather either by wrapping a nice warm blanket around them or preferably growing in a large container that can be brought inside during the winter.

Generally lemons are grown in containers in the UK and similar climates. They need a sunny spot when they are outside during the summer. Lemon trees make attractive and practical patio container plants.

Choose a healthy plant from your local garden supplier and check through the manufacturer's growing recommendations before you start as different hybrid varieties will have different requirements.

Lemons

If you are growing your lemon tree in a container it should be large enough to accommodate the tree's growth but it also needs to be transportable so that you can wheel it inside during the winter. There are trolleys you can buy for moving large containers. Prepare in advance so you don't strain your muscles trying to move an awkward and heavy pot.

Growing lemon trees outside needs careful planning. The tree must be planted in a warm sunny spot out of wind tunnels and it must never be planted in a frost pocket or waterlogged soil. Choose a well-drained sunny spot and dig a large hole before planting. Plant your tree and fill with rich well-rotted manure or compost. Water the tree in well.

All lemons, whether container grown or out in the garden, need watering about once a week. Don't be tempted to water a little every day. They prefer to have a good drink once a week and then left. To get water to the roots faster, sink a plastic bottle with the bottom cut off into the ground next to your lemon plant. Leave the cap on the bottle, unscrew and water well once a week, then screw the cap back on to prevent the bottle getting clogged with leaves or stones.

Some growers believe you should pick off the young immature fruits as they appear for the first two years. This is painful, when you really want your lemons to develop, but it can help to strengthen the plant for better harvests in subsequent years.

There are a number of new resistant strains of lemon trees available but there are a few pests and diseases to which lemons are susceptible, so watch out for any mould, aphids or leaves dropping. If treated quickly, most problems can be cleared up and your tree will go on to live a full life!

Bring indoors during the cold weather and always put out in the warm sun when the weather improves and your lemon tree will thrive.

Eating lemons

Lemons are one of those kitchen ingredients, like garlic, that no good chef would be without. Even if you don't consider yourself to be a particularly good chef, a little lemon juice in the right places can win you lots of brownie points in the kitchen.

HOMEMADE LEMONADE

This is a quick recipe that you can make at home. No fizz though! Roughly chop three whole (unwaxed) lemons and put them into a food processor with around 6 oz (140 g) of caster sugar and 1 pt (0.5 l) of cold water. Blend until the lemons are finely chopped. Sieve into a large bowl, pressing as much juice as you can through the sieve. Top up with another pint of water and serve. Chill or add ice cubes.

LEMON MERINGUE PIE

This is probably one of the more well-known lemon desserts, although there are plenty more. Buy or make 6 oz of short-crust pastry and roll it out to fit an 8 in (20 cm) tin. Lightly grease the tin if necessary and line with the pastry.

Chill for 30 minutes. Then bake the pastry case 'blind' by placing greaseproof paper on the pastry and putting a layer of dried beans on top. Bake in a preheated oven (Gas Mark 6, 400°F, 200°C) for about 15 minutes. Remove beans and greaseproof paper and pop back into the oven for 5 minutes to set.

Put the finely grated rind and juice of two lemons in a heavy-based saucepan with 4 oz (100 g) of granulated sugar and heat gently, stirring until the sugar is dissolved. In a small bowl, mix 3 oz (75 g) of cornflour with around 6 tbsp (90 ml) of water to make a smooth paste. Stir this paste into the lemon mixture and bring to the boil, stirring to blend well. Boil for about a minute until the mixture thickens. Remove from the heat and cool for a few minutes. Beat in two egg yolks, one at a time. Pour this warm filling into the pastry case, and level off.

Whisk two egg whites until stiff, then whisk in about 1.5 oz (40 g) of caster sugar until well mixed, then gently fold in another 1.5 oz (40 g) of caster sugar. Spoon meringue onto the filling and smooth over with a palette knife. Or use the point of a knife to flick up the meringue into peaks. Bake in a cool oven (Gas Mark 2, 300°F, 150°C) for around 35 minutes. Serve hot or cold with cream.

MEDITERRANEAN POTATOES

Although this is a potato dish, the lemon juice makes the potatoes come alive. Peel the potatoes and cut into 1–2 in (2.5–5 cm) chunks. Steam or boil until just cooked, then drain. Put a tablespoon of olive oil into a pan and gently fry chopped peppers, courgettes and an onion until tender. Stir in a handful of fresh herbs and the potatoes and cook for a couple of minutes. Then add the juice of one lemon and cook for another minute. Serve hot.

MORE LEMON IDEAS

- Cut lemons into wedges and serve with all fish dishes.

- Squeeze lemon juice on salads and other green vegetables.

- Add a slice to your favourite drink. A slice of lemon in a glass of water makes those eight glasses of water a day a lot more enjoyable.

- Squeeze a little lemon juice on cut apples to stop them going brown before cooking. This is really helpful if you are preparing a lot of windfall apples for a pie.

- Make a homemade lemon sorbet.

Lemons look very attractive in a fruit bowl but remember to use them in the kitchen as often as possible.

CHAPTER 6
DELICIOUS BLOOMS

Flowers have been used as decoration for thousands of years – in the home, in wedding and christening celebrations as well as in a garnish for food. Flowers are not only decorative, many of them are a good source of nutrition and can be eaten and enjoyed!

There are, of course, blooms and plants that are highly toxic. But as long as you can recognise the flowers you are growing and using, then there is no problem with eating them. The same applies to fungi. There are some wonderful species of wild fungi that are perfectly safe to eat – but there are others that are fatal.

Generally the petals of flowers are the best part to consume and it is advisable to remove the parts that join to the stem as these are often quite bitter in taste.

Grow your own edible flowers and garnish everyday meals. It's amazing how a few nasturtium or chive flowers brighten up the plainest green salad, and add a unique taste that the whole family will love!

Never consume flowers picked from the side of the road, or those bought from a florist, unless you are sure they haven't been sprayed with chemicals. They could have high levels of toxins.

This chapter covers six delicious blooms:

- dandelions

- marigolds

- nasturtiums

- roses

- violets.

There are plenty more that can be eaten:

- Courgette flowers are a delicacy. Try them dipped in batter and fried.

- Flowers from chive plants can be added to salads.

- Broccoli flowers are also edible.

Always make certain you know what you are eating as not all flowers are suitable for human consumption.

DANDELIONS

About dandelions

Dandelions are a very strong diuretic and should not be taken internally too near to bedtime! They are also a common weed considered by many gardeners to be a nuisance. However, nature tends to provide what we need and the common dandelion is a very useful plant. Like the lawn daisy, dandelions also have entertainment value. Children love to blow the seed 'clocks', counting each puff to find out what time it is, or whether 'she loves me' or 'she loves me not'.

Dandelions are a versatile plant. If your garden gets over-run with them, treat them as gifts rather than weeds. The flower heads can be used to make jam in place of fruit, the young leaves can be added to the salad bowl and have a high vitamin C content. The root can be roasted and ground to make a very acceptable substitute for coffee and the milky sap inside the stem is an effective cure for warts and verucas. Every single part of a dandelion plant is useful, which is probably why nature provides them in such abundance!

Growing dandelions

To be honest, dandelions shouldn't need cultivating but if you want to grow a large quantity for jam making, grab some seed and plant in a sunny spot. Keep watered but make sure they are not waterlogged. Dandelions are considered to be weeds by most gardeners and will usually re-seed and come up all over the place.

If, for some reason, dandelions don't come of their own accord in your garden, you may have to look elsewhere and wait for the seed head to appear, after flowering. Only collect from farmer's fields if you can be sure the ground is free of chemicals. And never collect from the side of the road because of car and animal pollution.

Dandelion seed isn't easy to buy, although some specialist seed suppliers may be able to help.

If the plants come up in your vegetable plot, dig up the root and re-plant or throw on the compost heap. Try and catch them when they are small as they have a long tap root and take hold fairly quickly. Don't leave them to grow in

Dandelion

your vegetable patch as they will re-seed and soon take over, drawing valuable nutrients from the soil and depriving your other crops. But if you can leave a couple to produce seed, then you can re-direct them next year.

Generally dandelions will grow in any soil type, even the poorest, but if you can provide a nice fertile sunny spot and look after them for a while, your crop will be better. Dig over a patch beforehand and dig in some well-rotted manure or fresh compost and remove any large stones and non-organic debris. Rake the ground over to a fine tilth and if you have seed scatter over the prepared bed and gently tamp down with the back of a rake. Watch that the birds don't find the seeds.

Dandelions will rarely need watering, only in very long dry spells. Their long tap root finds water before other plants will.

Many gardeners will probably think you are crazy, but most gardeners are slightly crazy themselves anyway, so take no notice! Dandelions are a great plant to grow and should be used as much as possible.

Eating dandelions

You really can use every part of the dandelion plant. The root is commercially grown as a substitute for coffee, and has been used for generations as the main ingredient in dandelion and burdock wines and cordials.

DANDELION GREENS

Dandelion leaves can be eaten like spinach or any spring greens. So if you are ever in the wilderness without food, look for the hardy dandelion to sustain you!

Put washed leaves in a saucepan and just cover with water. Bring to the boil, then reduce the heat and simmer until the leaves are tender. Drain well and chop finely. Serve hot. Dandelion leaves can also be steamed. Add a few chopped fresh herbs, or other seasoning to your taste, during cooking.

If the cooked leaves are bitter, drain well, add fresh water and a small spoonful of sugar and re-cook for a few minutes.

SALAD LEAVES

Use young fresh dandelion leaves in salads. Avoid the older larger leaves as they tend to taste bitter. Finely slice leaves and toss them into a green salad and add a dressing.

STIR-FRY

Finely sliced leaves can also be added in the last few seconds of cooking a stir-fry. Again only use young leaves.

DANDELION JAM

This old traditional French recipe for making dandelion jam requires you to collect exactly 365 dandelion flowers, on the first day you see them all over the fields and gardens. I've tried this recipe with 365 flowers and it worked beautifully, but when I tried to double the recipe it didn't!

Collect your flowers and rinse them carefully, then dry them. Use them as you would use fruit in a fruit jam recipe (for example, see the blackberry and apple jam recipe in Chapter 5) but add the grated rind and juice of a couple of oranges and a lemon to the flowers at the beginning of cooking.

Add sugar after cooking then bring the mixture to the setting point. You can either strain the dandelion mixture before adding sugar, or push the mixture through a sieve at the end. When the setting point has been reached, pour the jam into prepared warm jars. Label and store out of direct light. This recipe will only make a couple of small pots, so it's likely to be eaten before you have time to store it.

DANDELION COFFEE
Scrub dandelion roots and roast until cooked through. Leave to cool and then grind to make a substitute for coffee. Although to coffee drinkers this tastes nothing like coffee and is a poor substitute for the taste, it is a healthy drink as it is full of vitamins and minerals and seriously lacking in caffeine.

MARIGOLDS

About marigolds
Marigold is easily recognisable and a very popular garden plant. It tends to be fairly hardy and therefore easy to grow. There are many different varieties of marigold, but if you stick to the basic *calendula officinalis* you will be sure of having an edible plant that contains many vitamins and has a great taste.

Calendula officinalis, or pot marigold, is best to use in meals as other varieties have very dense petals, are usually hybrid varieties and can be lacking in vitamins. If you are going to eat a flower, it may as well be a highly nutritious one!

Marigolds have been grown over many centuries as a healing herb to soothe the nerves. They can be infused as a tea or added to soups, as well as mixed in with lotions to help the healing of wounds. The petals will make an effective homemade dye. Marigolds have also been used as a hair tonic.

Growing marigolds

Marigolds like a sunny position and will grow well along borders, in flowerbeds or even dotted about in the vegetable plot.

Sow seeds in well-drained pots or trays of seed compost in early spring. Keep them inside the house or in a greenhouse. Keep the soil moist and warm until the plants are ready to put outside. In warmer climates seed can be sown directly outside in rows. Thin plants when they are a few inches (5–8 cm) high, allowing about 9 in (20–25 cm) of space all round to grow.

Apart from keeping them free of weeds, marigolds shouldn't need any other attention. If the weather is unusually dry, water the plants a little but normally spring is damp and marigolds will thrive on their own in the early months of the year. If you are starting your plants off inside, it is a good idea to water

Marigolds

regularly until the plants are ready to be put out in the garden. Keep the compost damp but not too wet.

Although marigolds need little maintenance, watch out for slugs. Protect your plants, especially when they are young, from slugs and snails by any organic method you can find.

Use the flowers as you need them in the kitchen or to brighten up the house with small posies in bowls or vases. Marigolds are a curious plant as they produce many flowering branches from the main flowering stem. Picking regularly seems to encourage more growth and more blooms.

The flowers will bloom right through the summer, coming out in the morning and closing at night. Leave a few flowers to develop on the plants and they will self-seed, giving you a bed full of beautiful orange flowers next year without lifting a finger. If the winter is extremely cold, seed may not survive in the ground all year. Try to save a few by placing a piece of card or cloth around the plants when the seed starts to develop and catch the seeds as they fall. Failing that, you will have to plant marigold seed every year.

Eating marigolds

The bright orange marigold petals are a wonderful addition to all sorts of meals. Marigolds have been used to colour cheese in the past, and can be added to homemade cheeses to improve the colour and to add a little extra *je ne sais quoi* to your recipe. Marigolds are also used in bread making.

The marigold has long been considered a useful healing herb, as well as being employed in the kitchen usually in the form of a garnish. The leaves are also edible and can be added to salads, if you like the taste. Use only the young leaves.

Pick flowers just before you need them if possible, but always on the same day of eating. Gently pull apart the petals from the flower head and use them in the following ways:

- Stir carefully into a cold rice salad.

- Sprinkle into the salad bowl and stir in gently, or use as a garnish.

- Stir in to stir-fries after cooking.

- Stir into hot cooked rice to add the illusion of saffron!

- Sprinkle petals over chocolate or lemon cakes and gateaux.

- Garnish fruit salads and ice creams.

- Use the bright colours to add imagination and flair to everyday meals.

Whole blooms can be used to garnish:

- green or other mixed salads

- elaborate fruit desserts

- the dinner table. A single flower on side plates takes little effort but is very effective.

Marigold petals are a beautiful, bright orange colour and will compliment most food displays or individual dishes. Don't forget to use them. Small posies in vases or bowls add a touch of elegance to a dinner party.

NASTURTIUMS

About nasturtiums

Nasturtiums are a hardy, self-seeding herb that will cover a whole bed if not checked. Plant one or two nasturtium plants in between vegetables as they repel the bad insects and encourage the good guys! Little data is available about the properties of nasturtiums, although they are known to have a high vitamin C content. The flowers and leaves have a peppery taste similar to watercress.

Nasturtium flowers have been used as a culinary flower and herb for centuries. They are a trailing vine and can be grown as ground cover or trained to climb over a trellis to create a flowering fence or border. They are an attractive addition to a herb garden and can also be grown in pots on a patio or balcony.

The flowers, leaves and seeds can all be used in the kitchen and should be! Nasturtium seeds are a good substitute for the more expensive caper, which is an important pickling spice. Seed can be collected and stored for use in the kitchen or planted the following year.

Growing nasturtiums

Nasturtiums are classified as a herb and are probably one of the easiest plants to grow in your garden. They can be trained to climb fences or left as good ground cover. The foliage is fairly dense which helps to discourage weeds. It is a good plant to have in the vegetable garden, although it does tend to re-seed itself, and in areas where there hasn't been a heavy frost they are likely to come up on their own year after year. Don't feed the soil unless it is very poor. Nasturtiums will produce lots of leaf but little flower in very rich soil.

They can be started from seed early in the year. Fill well-drained trays or pots with potting compost, and plant two or three seeds per pot or thinly in a tray.

Nasturtiums grow quickly though and, rather than taking up valuable space in the greenhouse or conservatory, it's just as good to wait a couple of months and sow directly outside.

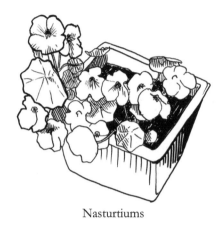

Nasturtiums

Wait until all danger of frost has passed then dig over the ground and remove any perennial weeds or non-organic debris. Rake to a fine tilth. Then sow seeds 8–12 in (20–30 cm) apart. The seeds are large and easy to handle.

Nasturtiums are also a good container plant. They do need a lot of water though, so pots should never be allowed to dry out. All containers and pots must be well drained.

Fix up a trellis or some hooks onto a fence if you want the plants to climb. As they grow you will probably have to help them find their way but, once they get going, very little needs doing apart from making sure they get enough water.

With a little careful planning you may only ever have to buy one packet of nasturtium seeds. When the seeds start to appear on your plants, lay a sheet of card or cloth under the plants to collect them as they drop. Leave these seeds to dry indoors for a day then put them into a jar for planting next year or using in the kitchen. In some areas, nasturtiums will re-seed themselves and come up year after year.

Eating nasturtiums

There's a lot of food value in a nasturtium plant. The flowers, leaves and seed are all usable in the kitchen. The seeds can be used to replace capers in pickling spice.

PICKLING

Add nasturtium seeds to white wine vinegar and leave for a few weeks before using so that the flavour seeps into the vinegar. Seeds can be bruised or broken for a stronger or faster effect. The vinegar should be strained if broken seeds are used.

LEAVES

Nasturtium leaves can be shredded or chopped finely and added to:

- green salads. Toss into a bowl with mixed shredded lettuce, then add other ingredients. Nasturtium leaves have a peppery taste and should be used in moderation with milder tasting foods.

- stir-fries. Finely slice or chop the leaves and add to stir-fry ingredients in the last minute or two of the cooking time.

Leaves can also be chopped finely and used to garnish soups or other dishes.

FLOWERS

Nasturtium flowers make a very elegant garnish. They always add a touch of sophistication to a dinner table.

- Throw a few on top of a salad.

- Place a single flower on side plates.

- Arrange different coloured nasturtium flowers around a main dish just before serving.

- Use flowers to decorate a special occasion cake. Flowers taste peppery like the leaves so it may be advisable not to eat the flowers with a mouthful of cake!

And there's nothing to stop you livening up the taste buds while you are pottering in the garden! Young nasturtium leaves are very high in vitamin C and are a good food to pick and eat while wandering in the garden.

ROSES

About roses

There are over ten thousand different varieties of rose – many people make a lifetime study of this wonderful flower and spend years creating new varieties. What a magical job!

Most roses are edible and can be used in decorations and flavourings in the kitchen. The dog rose, often found growing wild, produces rose hips that contain more vitamin C gram for gram than oranges. The dog rose is a hardy plant and a useful one to grow now that many hedgerows have disappeared.

Rose hips were grown and collected during the war years and made into rose hip syrup, one of the most popular cordials around, as well as being a good source of vitamins, especially during those years when nutritious food was scarce. Many of us in the UK were brought up on rose hip syrup.

Roses are a passionate hobby for many people and there is always good advice to be found from local growers. They have been cultivated for over two thousand years and are known as the queen of flowers.

Growing roses

Roses can be started from seed but could take up to two years to germinate. They are usually propagated with cuttings. Rose trees of all varieties are available from most garden suppliers. Make sure your rose tree or shrub has recommended growing and planting instructions with it. Different varieties have different requirements.

Cuttings can be taken from an established plant. The best time to do this is at pruning time, after all the flowers have finished for the year. Trim your cuttings and only use the healthiest looking pieces. Cut them back to about 3 or 4 in (7–10 cm) and push them into pots of fresh compost. Water well after planting. Keep the soil damp but never too wet, and look after them until the cuttings have established roots and can be planted out into their permanent position.

Cuttings can be started in a seedbed but should be protected over the winter months with a cloche. Some cuttings may have developed roots the following spring but others may take a little longer.

New shoots are also used to propagate roses. Remove new shoots and plant them in fresh compost as with cuttings. Look after them until the roots have developed.

Rose

Dog roses are rambling plants and can be started by layering. Choose a healthy lower branch and push into the soil where it comfortably touches the ground. Secure with a V-shaped peg, cover with fresh compost then water. When the new plant has developed roots it can be cut from the mother plant and transplanted.

Roses are hardy woody plants and are generally easy to grow and maintain. Most rose varieties need pruning once a year. Take out any dead wood and overcrowding branches. Let the plant breathe.

Climbing roses can be trained to grow over any garden structure or on a fence or wall. Cut the plants back regularly to allow healthy growth and lots of flowers. Gently tie branches to hooks or weave them through trellises or other structures.

Check on manufacturer's growing recommendations for any further advice when buying hybrid varieties of rose. Grow a dog rose in a 'wild' part of the garden to bring a splash of colour and encourage bees and other wildlife to the garden. Although dog roses grow wild in some rural areas, it is a useful plant to grow and can be more or less left to its own devices.

Eating roses

Roses are considered to be a herb and are very practical to grow in the home garden. Apart from the single rose or extravagant bouquet gracing a dinner table, the leaves and fruits are also usable.

FLOWERS

Rose flowers are used to decorate gateaux and other desserts. Generally small roses, such as the tea rose, are used for decoration and can be frosted. To frost flowers, dip the top of the flower very gently into beaten egg white then into fine sugar. Leave to dry.

The petals can be scattered over large desserts or a couple of petals arranged on individual helpings. Rose petals are useful for flavouring food. Add petals to the blender when mixing ice creams or cakes.

LEAVES
Rose leaves make an enjoyable herbal tea. Pour boiling water on a few leaves in a jug. Cover and leave to infuse for about five minutes then strain and drink.

ROSE HIPS
Rose hips are the fruits of the rose plant and, gram for gram, are higher in vitamin C content than citrus fruits. Use them! Rose hips have been made into cordials for generations and can be added to homemade country wines.

Cut rosehips and remove the seeds, then simmer in a little water until soft. Mash and sieve or put through a blender. Use the remaining puree as a concentrate for:

- Making juices and wines. Add hot water and a little sugar and lemon juice if liked. Leave for a few minutes for the flavours to absorb before straining. Drink immediately or leave to cool and chill. For wines, rose hips can be added with the grapes or other fruit.

- Blending into ice cream or other desserts.

This blend of beautiful displays and useful flavourings puts roses in the 'must-grow' category in the garden!

VIOLETS

About violets
In some rural areas, wild violets can still be found at the right time of year. They flower in late winter or early spring but tend to be very shy, often

growing well hidden amongst other wild flowers or grassland. Look out for them in the spring around your local parks and woodland. Once established, violets make good ground cover only growing to 3 or 4 in (7–10 cm) in height.

Violets have been cultivated as a medicinal herb for at least 2,500 years and are still used today in many herbal preparations across the world. The delicate flowers are candied and used to decorate celebration cakes and other desserts. Violets have a very distinct flavour and once tried can't be forgotten. The flowers and leaves are edible.

Violet leaves have expectorant qualities and can alleviate bronchial symptoms. They have also been found to aid in curing certain types of cancer. The flowers and leaves have mild laxative properties and therefore shouldn't be taken in large doses. Violets, being woodland plants, like a semi-shady position so will do well in a part of the garden where the sun doesn't shine all the time.

Growing violets

Growing violets from seed can be erratic at best but is possible. Seed should be started in well-drained pots or trays of fresh compost. The compost should be kept damp but not waterlogged. Germination can take some time. Although violets tolerate low temperatures, at this stage they need to be kept warm. Keep trays and pots in a warm conservatory or greenhouse, if possible, or in a warm bright place indoors. Check for any manufacturer's growing recommendations on the seed packet.

Keep warm and watered until seedlings are large enough to handle and all danger of frost has passed before planting out in their permanent position in the garden. Allow about 12 in (30 cm) of space between plants.

The quickest way to get a violet bed under way is to buy plants from your garden supplier or a local grower. *Viola odorata* is the species known as 'sweet violets' and is probably the best one to grow if possible.

Choose a fairly shady spot in the garden for your plants. They will grow in a sunny position but tend to dry out too quickly. Many flowering plants need a sunny spot so violets are an ideal plant to fill a shady area. They are a good ground cover and also flower early in the year before the summer blooms take over.

Dig over the ground before planting and remove any large stones, non-organic debris and perennial weeds.

In the autumn, new plants can be propagated from the old. There are three ways you can do this:

- Runners: Violets send out runners like strawberry plants and will replant themselves given the right conditions. Otherwise carefully remove plants from the main plant and re-plant somewhere else.

- Root division: Dig carefully around the plants and lift them out of the ground. Separate the roots and re-plant pieces immediately into pots or containers until the following spring. Put them out in the garden when they are growing well.

Violets

- Cuttings: Take cuttings from healthy plants and push into pots of fresh compost. Keep indoors or protect from the cold during the winter. Plant out in the following autumn when the cuttings have developed roots.

Violet plants are evergreen and the leaves can be used all year round.

Eating violets

Pick violets for use when they bloom. Pick them carefully so you don't pull up the whole plant. The flowering season doesn't last long so the more you grow the better. The leaves stay green all year and can be used anytime.

FLOWERS

Violet flowers can be used in the following ways.

- Add to salads. Toss gently into a green salad or use to garnish any mixed salad. The violet flowers colour the dish and add an extra special taste.

- Infuse to make tea. Simply pour boiling water over a few violets in a jug and leave to steep for five minutes. Strain and drink while still hot. Dried flowers can be used to make tea, so if you have too many to use in the spring dry a few for the winter months. Hang them upside down until crisp then gently put into jars and keep out of direct light.

- Crystallise to decorate celebration cakes and elaborate desserts. Or rather than going through the whole crystallising process, frost the flowers instead. Dip tips of flowers in beaten egg white then in sugar. Leave to dry before using.

- Scatter violets over a dinner table or collect small bunches and arrange them in elegant bowls or vases.

LEAVES

Leaves can be used to make tea and also for adding flavour to any dish that could 'do with a touch of violets'.

CHAPTER 7

EGGSTRA SPECIAL

ALL ABOUT EGGS

Eggs are nutritious, versatile and relatively inexpensive. They are a lean protein food and are useful in our everyday diets. They also contain traces of many minerals and all of the following vitamins:

- A

- D

- E

- B12

- biotin

- choline

- folic acid (folacin)

- niacin

- pantothenic acid

- pyridoxine (B6)

- riboflavin (B2)

- thiamine (B1)

Eggs are nutritious, low in fat – one whole medium egg contains around 75 to 80 calories – and can be enjoyed in so many different ways. There are plenty of recipe ideas in this chapter although we would need a whole book to include all the possible recipes you can experiment with if you have an egg or two in the fridge.

Of course, all being well with local authority rules and regulations, you could even keep a few laying hens in your back garden, giving you fresh organic eggs every day as well as the possibility of hatching your own baby chicks in time for Easter.

KEEPING HENS

Although hens are originally woodland birds, they are very happy scratching around on a patch of grassland. There are a few things to take into account before embarking on keeping hens. Firstly, you should check with local authority rules and regulations just in case there are restrictions in your area over keeping poultry.

There is no national law against keeping poultry but if you have a noisy cockerel or the area becomes dirty or smelly, there could be a nuisance issue to deal with. Keeping the birds clean and healthy is a must and if you have a very noisy cockerel, you could try keeping him inside a little later in the morning. It isn't necessary to keep a cockerel to keep your hens laying but if you do want one, there are quieter breeds available. The Poultry Club has a list

Hens on grassland

of breeds on their website – www.poultryclub.org – as well as a helpful advice centre.

Always buy your poultry from a reputable supplier. Bantams are a popular breed as they are generally good layers and are smaller than average. They lay smaller eggs but six bantams will normally provide four to six eggs a day.

Secondly, be sure you have time for them. Keeping hens is fairly low maintenance but you do have to feed them, shut them in at night and let them out in the morning. Their coop also needs to be cleaned out regularly.

When you have the green light and are sure you can organise their upkeep, the following pointers should help get you going.

Space

Although some books advise that you should allow a square metre of land for every hen you keep, I prefer to give them a bit more space than that. Keeping them happy will encourage them to lay more eggs. If you want to fatten them for eating then restricting their exercise and limiting their space would be advisable.

If you are keeping hens on a patch of grass, they will inevitably scratch it down to the earth within three to six months depending on the condition of the soil and the size and number of your hens. Dividing a patch into sections and moving the hens between them every couple of months will give the soil time to replenish and the grass time to grow back.

Alternatively, you can keep hens on hard ground but they should be given supplements as they won't be scratching for bugs. The area will also need to be cleaned regularly.

However you keep your hens, it's a good idea to enclose the space with chicken wire to keep them safe from other animals, especially foxes, and also to keep your vegetable plot safe. Hens can destroy a newly sown seedbed in seconds and they will also probably eat the seeds.

Housing

You can buy chicken houses all ready made with nesting boxes and perches. But an old shed can easily be turned into a chicken house. A large space isn't necessary for birds to sleep in – they tend to cuddle up together anyway. The chicken house should be ventilated at the top, and any other holes patched up to deter rats and mice.

Nesting boxes should be provided. Laying areas should be just big enough for the birds to stand up in as well as lay their eggs. A purpose-built chicken house will have a lift up lid so you can remove the eggs easily after the hens have laid them.

Fresh straw is advisable for nesting and keeping your hens warm at night. Renew the straw regularly. The cleaner the housing, the better for the hens' welfare and egg production.

Food

Hens that are kept on grass during the day or allowed to roam free through trees will need very little extra food. A handful of corn will encourage them to lay and specially produced pellets can be bought from farm and garden supply shops if you feel they could do with a little extra boost.

Hens kept on hard ground should be given corn and laying pellets, and it's a good idea to give them excess produce from the garden such as lettuces, vegetable peelings, pumpkin and melon seeds. They will peck over many different foods. Give them the caterpillars you pick off the cabbages in the vegetable garden.

Collecting eggs from your own garden along with a few vegetables creates a wonderful feeling of freedom. A whole meal from your own land ... no shopping, cheque books or cash involved, no car drive and very little time involved in bringing the food to the table.

Of course, keeping hens will cost a bit. But the initial costs are far outweighed by the fresh eggs you can collect every day for years to come. Most hens will only lay for about three years, but some go on and on.

If you keep a cockerel your eggs will be fertilised and when one of the hens gets broody she may just hatch out a new brood of hens ready to grow and become new layers – well some of them, you may have to give away or roast the cockerels.

If you have young children, they will be delighted with the tiny fluffy chicks. All in all, keeping hens is a great thing to do but does require a certain amount of time and input. Get to know your hens and they will lay an egg a day nearly all year round.

COOKING WITH EGGS

Savoury dishes

The following few recipes are all variations on omelettes. The possibilities are endless though so get imaginative with those leftovers!

TOASTED EGG SANDWICH

Beat an egg until bubbly and pour into a hot pan with a little frying oil. Sprinkle on a little grated cheese or crumbled feta cheese and cook for a couple of minutes each side.

Place between two slices of hot buttered toast. This is a satisfying snack and fairly low in calories if you don't use butter.

LEFTOVER SURPRISE

Stir-fry leftover chicken, bacon pieces, tuna chunks, mushrooms or anything you have to hand. When reheating meat, always make sure it is piping hot right through.

Beat a couple of eggs per person and pour over the mixture in the pan. Cook for a few minutes over a low to medium heat. Turn the omelette over and cook for a further two or three minutes. If it falls apart, just push it all back together.

MEAL-IN-A-PAN

Peel a medium-sized potato (one per person) and cut into cubes. Steam or boil until tender. Drain and set aside. Steam or boil a handful of fresh or frozen peas. Drain and set aside.

Cut or slice any mixture of the following ingredients (depending on what you have in the fridge):

- sweet pepper

- onion

- tomato

- courgette (zucchini)

- aubergine.

Stir-fry the vegetables for a couple of minutes. Then add the cooked potato and peas to the pan and mix well. Cook gently over a low heat for two or three minutes, stirring to prevent sticking.

Beat eggs well (allow two per person). Then pour the eggs over the vegetables in the pan. Cook thoroughly until the eggs are set, turning after a few minutes. Serve hot with a green salad.

PASTA BAKE

Boil a couple of eggs until hard-boiled (at least five minutes). Peel and chop roughly. Bring a large saucepan of water to the boil and add the pasta. Lower the heat and simmer until the pasta is cooked but not too soft. Drain well, allow to cool for a few minutes, then stir in the chopped boiled eggs.

Place the pasta and egg mixture into a casserole dish, sprinkle a little grated cheese on top and heat through in the oven or under the grill until the cheese has melted.

For variation, chopped ham, cooked bacon, chicken slices or tuna chunks can be added to the pasta and egg mixture before reheating. As mentioned before, always make sure meat is piping hot right through when reheating.

Before reheating the dish of pasta and eggs, stir in a béchamel, cheese or mushroom sauce. A simple mushroom sauce can be made by making up a packet of dried mushroom soup but using less water. Stir well to remove any lumps then gently fold into the pasta and eggs before reheating.

EGG CURRY

This is a simple every day curry dish. Hard boil your eggs (allowing two per person for a main meal, or one for a side dish or snack). Cool the eggs and peel. Cut in half lengthwise and arrange in an ovenproof dish.

Make or buy a simple curry sauce and pour over the eggs.

Place the dish in a pre-heated medium oven for about 20 minutes or until the sauce is cooked and the eggs are hot. Serve with basmati rice and accompany with fresh chopped onion, plain yoghurt, and a green salad as preferred.

UNE AMÉRICAIN

In France, *une américain* is a popular sandwich in many cafés and bars.

Fill a buttered baguette with slices of boiled egg, ham, lettuce and tomato. Add mayonnaise for authenticity or mustard if preferred. Very small baguettes or bridge rolls are an acceptable alternative to the long French baguette for packed lunches and quick snacks.

BOILED EGG WITH SOLDIERS

This has been a traditional breakfast for children and adults in the UK for many generations. Soft boil an egg for about 2.5 to 3.5 minutes depending on the size of the egg. Serve in a warmed egg cup with narrow strips of buttered bread or toast.

SCRAMBLED EGGS

Beat one or two eggs in a basin, add a little milk and stir well. Put a knob of butter in a small pan and gently heat until the butter has melted. Pour in the egg mixture and keep the heat very low. Stir with a wooden spoon until the eggs are set.

The eggs will continue to cook for a few seconds after the heat has been turned off, so if you don't like your eggs too well done, turn off the heat a little before the end of cooking. Stir well and serve on hot buttered toast.

Scrambled egg also cooks very successfully in a microwave. Simply beat eggs and milk in a microwave-able jug and cook for a minute or two depending on the power of the microwave. Stir halfway through the cooking time.

For variation, beat the eggs and add milk. Then add any of the following according to taste:

- half a teaspoon of ready-made mustard

- a little grated cheese or crumbled feta cheese

- some finely grated onion.

Stir well, then cook as before.

POACHED EGGS
Eggs can be poached either using a poacher or in the traditional way. Fill a medium saucepan halfway with water and bring to the boil. Add a few drops of vinegar according to taste, then carefully break the egg and drop into the boiling water. Hold the egg low over the pan to avoid splashing. Or break into a small cup or bowl first to make sure you haven't dropped any shell into the pan.

Bring the water back to the boil and simmer for two or three minutes – just long enough to toast a slice of bread. Use a slotted spoon to remove your poached egg from the water and serve on hot buttered toast. If you use a low fat spread instead of butter, poached egg on toast is a healthy and low calorie breakfast.

NO-GUILT BREAKFAST FRY-UP

Fry-ups have never been better. Poach your eggs and serve with grilled lean bacon rashers, grilled tomatoes and toast spread with a low fat alternative to butter. A fry-up with no frying and lots of protein will get you through the morning.

YORKSHIRE PUDDING

Originating from Yorkshire in the north of England, Yorkshire pudding has been solid fare against the cold weather for centuries. It used to be eaten before the main meal with a little meat gravy to take the edge off the appetite.

Ingredients

   4 oz (125 g) plain flour

   Pinch of salt

   1 egg

   7 fl oz (200 ml) milk

   Cooking oil

Method

1. Sieve the flour into a large bowl and add the salt.

2. Make a well in the centre of the flour and break an egg into it.

3. Add the milk a little at a time and keep stirring well with a wooden spoon. When all the milk has been added, beat well until the mixture leaves a few bubbles on the surface when still. If the mixture goes lumpy, try straining and then beating well.

4. Pour a tiny drop of oil into each compartment of a patty or tartlet tin (12 portions) and place in a pre-heated oven (Gas Mark 7, 425°F or 220°C) for 5 or 10 minutes until the oil is very hot.

5. Remove the tin from the oven and carefully pour in the batter, half filling each compartment.

6. Place in a hot oven as before and bake for 15–20 minutes. Serve hot with a Sunday roast – or eat cold with jams or jellies.

Desserts

CHOCOLATE DREAM CAKE

Although you *can* make an egg-less sponge cake – it's never quite the same. Try this wicked chocolate dream cake . . .

Ingredients

6 oz (150 g) self-raising flour

6 oz (150 g) chocolate powder

6 oz (150 g) sugar

4 oz (100 g) butter (or equivalent)

3 small eggs (beaten)

1 tsp baking powder

Method

1. Preheat the oven to Gas Mark 6, 400°F or 200°C and line a cake tin (8 or 9 inch/20–22 cm) with greaseproof paper.

2. Mix the flour and chocolate powder together in a bowl.

3. In a large mixing bowl, beat together the butter and sugar until light and fluffy.

4. Add the beaten egg a little at a time, beating well after each addition.

5. Fold in the flour and chocolate powder mixture, then finally the baking powder. Mix well.

6. Put the mixture into the prepared tin and bake for 30–40 minutes.

7. Turn out onto a wire tray to cool.

If you manage to keep the cake until it's cold – and good luck! – coat with a vanilla or coffee icing. Irresistible!

EGG CUSTARD

Whisk two eggs with 2 level tsp (30 ml) of sugar in a large bowl. Warm half a pint (300 ml) of milk in a pan but don't bring to the boil. Pour the milk over the eggs. Stir gently and pour into a lightly greased ovenproof dish. Sprinkle grated nutmeg on top.

Bake in a pre-heated oven at Gas Mark 7, 425°F or 220°C for 10 minutes then reduce the heat to Gas Mark 4, 380°F or 180°C. Bake for a further 20 minutes or until set. Remove from the oven and leave to cool. Serve cold.

CUSTARD TARTS

Egg custard can be poured into a large pastry case or smaller individual pastry cases. Line tins with pastry and bake 'blind' in a preheated oven at Gas Mark 6, 400°F or 200°C. To bake pastry 'blind', line a greased or non-stick tin with pastry and cover with a layer of greaseproof paper. Put a layer or two of dried beans on top of the greaseproof paper and bake for about 8–10 minutes. This procedure 'sets' the pastry while preventing it from rising.

Remove the tins from the oven and take the beans and paper from the pastry cases. Cool for at least five minutes then pour the custard mixture into the pastry cases. Bake for about 50 minutes at Gas Mark 6, 400°F or 200°C for a large custard tart or reduce the cooking time to about 20–30 minutes for smaller tarts. When the custard has set, the tarts are ready.

PANCAKES

To make pancakes use exactly the same batter mix as for Yorkshire pudding (see page 168). Leave the batter to stand for 30 minutes in a cold place, then stir well before cooking.

Heat a little oil in a frying pan until hot. Pour in a large tablespoon of batter, and swirl the pan until the batter thins and spreads evenly over the base. Cook for a minute or two, then turn and cook the other side for a couple of minutes.

Traditionally pancakes are served hot with a squeeze of lemon and a little sugar. Or spread strawberry jam or chocolate spread thinly over the pancake. Roll up and serve whilst still warm.

Eggstra tips

- Use free-range eggs whenever possible or keep a few laying hens.

- Don't store eggs in too cold a temperature. If you have a cold larder they are better kept in there than the fridge. Although if your hens have been laying too many to keep up with, keep them in the bottom part of the fridge until you can use them. Alternatively give your spare eggs away.

- Don't worry about eggs being bad for you, unless you have a particular intolerance. Eggs are nutritious, high in protein and low in fat.

- Having an egg for breakfast really does fill you up for longer and will definitely help if you are on a calorie controlled diet.

- As we get older, our bone mass reduces and we need to keep up our calcium levels. Many adults don't like to drink milk, but eggs are a great substitute.

- Eggs are relatively cheap and they can make a good mid-week meal for all the family.

- Always add eggs a little at a time to sponge cakes. The mixture may curdle otherwise. If you have a food processor, all the ingredients can be whizzed together at the same time.

- Break eggs into a small bowl or cup before adding to your recipe to avoid any small pieces of shell ending up in your dish.

- When a recipe requires eggs to be beaten, use a fork or a small hand whisk and beat well until bubbly.

CHAPTER 8

AROUND THE HOUSE

Generally eating five portions of fruit and veg every day will keep skin soft, organs working well and provide a general sense of well-being. However, many of the delicious fruits, vegetables and herbs found in this book can be used for other things as well as simply eating . . .

FROM CHAPTER 1 – THE SALAD BOWL

Tomatoes

As well as being one of the most versatile foods to grow, tomatoes have been the subject of many scientific studies and have been proven to be strong antioxidants, helping to reduce the risk of certain cancers. They are also unique in that they not only retain their healthy properties after cooking, but some are also improved.

Tomatoes are a good deodoriser. To eliminate stale smells from a fridge, wipe undiluted tomato juice around the inside, then rinse and dry. Tomato juice can also be used to deodorise your dog after a smelly woodland walk. Sponge undiluted tomato juice all over your dog, avoiding his or her eyes, and wait a few minutes. Then shampoo or scrub with soap and water.

For many years tomatoes have been used as non-harmful weapons during rural festivals!

Lettuce

Lettuce has been cultivated for thousands of years and was believed to be sacred by the Ancient Egyptians. Lettuce has slightly sedative properties and although it has a cool refreshing taste, it can help calm and soothe the nerves. The Romans ate it after a meal to induce sleep.

Coarser lettuce leaves can be cooked as well as eaten raw. It is a low calorie, fat free food and is high in vitamins.

Cucumber

Cucumbers are a well-documented diuretic and very low in calories, making them a popular diet food.

They are a refreshing and cool vegetable and can reduce puffiness around the eyes. Lie back with a slice of cucumber over each closed eye for 15 minutes to get the full benefit. Slices of cucumber or cucumber juice can be gently dabbed onto sunburned skin to cool and soothe.

Peppers

Information about the use of peppers as a direct cosmetic or medicinal treatment is hard to come by. However, due to their vitamin, mineral and dietary fibre content, they are a worthwhile ingredient in a healthy diet. They are also practical and versatile vegetables to cook with as well as being varied in colour, shape and size.

Onions

Onions come in a huge variety of shapes and sizes, and no good chef would be without them. However onions also have a diverse history of uses. During the Middle Ages they were used as currency to pay rent or given as gifts.

They have been proven to alleviate coughs and other flu symptoms. Slice or chop an onion and sprinkle with a spoonful of sugar. Leave in a covered bowl overnight. The following morning, the liquid residue, which should be sipped, will soothe coughs and sore throats.

Cut an onion in half and apply to a bee or wasp sting to reduce the swelling and relieve the soreness.

It is also believed that if you eat a lot of onions, mosquitoes go in search of sweeter blood. This is probably where the warding off Dracula idea came from.

FROM CHAPTER 2 – DOWN TO ROOTS

Carrots

Carrots come in many colours although white carrots will be lacking in the carotenes found in orange or red varieties. Carotenes turn into vitamin A in the body and, as a deficiency in vitamin A is known to cause poor vision, there is some truth in the rumour about carrots improving your night vision!

Carrot juice has long been sold as a health drink and can be made at home in a blender or juicer. Carrots are high in dietary fibre and minerals and are a versatile and tasty addition to the daily diet.

Beetroot

Beetroot has been used in medicinal preparations since Roman times and was considered to be an aphrodisiac. The roots contain an element known as boron, which stimulates the sex hormones.

Beetroot juice has been shown in studies to significantly reduce blood pressure and is therefore a useful food for high blood pressure sufferers. Preliminary studies are also showing that beetroot aids in protecting the liver from fatty deposits caused by alcohol or other toxin build up.

Beetroot is used commercially for colouring many different food products including tomato sauce as well as desserts, jellies and jams.

Parsnips

Parsnips are very rich in potassium and high in dietary fibre, making them a good food to include in a healthy diet. They have also been used for many years as a digestive aid.

Parsnip can be mashed and given to babies to soothe and alleviate wind pain.

They can be used in sweet dishes as well as cooked as an everyday vegetable.

Salsify

Salsify is another nutritious vegetable, being high in minerals including iron, calcium and potassium. It also contains a number of beneficial vitamins. The high level of fructose in salsify makes it a good vegetable for diabetics.

Potatoes

Potatoes are not only versatile in the kitchen, they can also be utilised in a number of other areas around the house.

Cut a potato in half and carve out a design to make a 'stamp' for the kids to paint with. Use thick poster paints for bright colours.

Rub a raw potato over hands after cutting carrots or beetroot to remove staining.

Cut a raw potato into thick slices and arrange around a houseplant that has been suffering from worms in the roots. The worms are attracted to the potato and leave your plant alone!

Potatoes have also been used in the past as a cleaner for shoes, ornaments and various other household items. Rub the potato flesh over area and rinse afterwards.

FROM CHAPTER 3 – EVERYDAY VEG

Peas

Apart from the common 'pea soup' reference to the heavy fogs that tended to rest over cities up until the mid twentieth century, peas are best known for eating!

Many cultures across the world have traditionally made pea soup according to their regional varieties. A pot of pea soup would often be bubbling on the stove for many days.

Peas are one of the most useful vegetables through the winter months as they freeze and dry well.

Beans

As regular green beans, there's not much to be done with them apart from eating. However if you dry a few of the mature beans inside the pods, they can be used for all sorts of things.

Use dried beans to bake your pastry 'blind'. Lay beans on greaseproof paper on top of your pastry case to prevent the pastry from rising.

Beans can be used for counters in board games where the real pieces went walkabout ages ago. They can also be used to play 'jacks'. Traditionally played with stones, the game involves scattering between five and ten beans on the ground, then throwing one bean up in the air and trying to gather all the others – or one of them at a time – before the thrown 'bean' is caught again. All of this needs to be done using the same one hand.

Try making bean bags. Sew two squares of strong cloth together and fill with beans before sewing the last seam. Small bean bags make great toys for kids and larger ones are ideal comfy cushions or footstools.

Broccoli

Broccoli flowers are a useful food garnish and, like the vegetable itself, broccoli seed is known to have a very high vitamin content. Growing broccoli sprouts, that is, eating the very young plants before they really start to grow, is becoming popular among health enthusiasts.

Asparagus

Asparagus is often highly priced in shops making it worth growing just for the touch of luxury in your back garden. It has been cultivated for many years as an edible vegetable and has also been proven to have some effect in curing kidney problems.

Asparagus is well known as an 'aphrodisiac' although this could be due to the phallic shape rather than any particular mineral cocktail. Asparagus is low in sodium and high in dietary fibre.

Courgettes

Once you have them growing, keeping up with eating your courgettes can be a problem. The plants do stop producing their fruits at some point though, so make the most of your harvest and freeze a few courgette dishes for the winter.

Courgettes are a squash and as with most edible squashes the seeds are beneficial. They are said to keep the body free of intestinal parasites so can help prevent tummy bugs, especially when on holiday – although explaining the reason for the courgette seeds in your suitcase to customs officials at the airport could prove difficult!

FROM CHAPTER 4 – HERB CORNER

Basil

A pot of fresh basil growing near an open window or door will help repel flies during the summer months.

Move your pots into a warmer but light place at the end of the summer and they will keep growing for a while longer.

Basil has mild sedative properties and will help alleviate stomach cramps. An infusion of basil leaves sipped slowly can soothe headaches and relax the body.

Bay

Bay is a useful decorative plant during the winter and has traditionally been used in winter decorations for Christmas and other celebrations. Noblemen wore head-dresses of laurel as far back as Roman times. Get the children making centrepieces for the festive dinner table. Mix with holly and other evergreens for a spectacular display.

The oil from bay has powerful antiseptic qualities and is used in many commercial medicinal preparations.

Chives

Chives are a member of the onion family and have the same properties, albeit milder, than regular onions. Chives are a good replacement for onions especially in salads and with other raw foods. They will help alleviate cough and cold symptoms but the nutritional effects will be milder than with onions.

Coriander

In the past, coriander was believed to bestow immortality. Although this is clearly a myth, coriander has been used in many medicinal preparations and treatments over the ages and is still accepted today as being a useful aid in digestion. Use leaves and seeds in everyday dishes to relieve pain from indigestion.

Coriander has a very strong aroma and, like other herbs, will help deter pests from your vegetable garden.

Fennel

Fennel, with its aniseed-like flavour, provides one of the best digestive aids of the everyday herbs you can grow. It has long been considered to be a valuable addition to a weight loss diet. Although fennel does in fact stimulate the appetite, it also helps to digest food more efficiently. It has also been effective in alleviating cold and flu symptoms.

Like other aromatic herbs, fennel's strong smell will deter pests from your garden.

Garlic

Garlic really has stood the test of time as a healing herb and has been cultivated for medicinal and culinary use for thousands of years. Garlic has strong antibiotic properties making it an excellent cleansing food. It also has significant amounts of dietary fibre and vitamins. And of course if you hang some garlic over your front door you will never be troubled with vampires again!

Chew parsley leaves with or after eating garlic to freshen the breath. Garlic shouldn't be taken in large doses by those suffering from eczema as it can aggravate the condition.

Mint

Mint is another ancient healing herb and, as well as being a must-have with roast lamb, it is an exceptional digestive aid. A cup of mint tea every day will soothe many digestive problems, including stomach cramps, irritable bowel syndrome and other general disorders. Mint tea can also relieve tension headaches without having to resort to painkillers.

Mint has been served as an after dinner food in the form of chocolate mints for many years with good reason!

Oregano

Oregano has been used for centuries as a food preserver. The anti-microbe compounds in oregano help destroy microbes that may be in meats and other foods.

Oregano aids digestion and is often used today in medicinal preparations to cure many minor ailments. A cup of oregano tea every day is packed with minerals and vitamins and will help ward off colds and flu.

Parsley

Parsley has been fashionably used as a garnish for many years but the true food value is now being recognised. Parsley is full of vitamins and nutrients and is a herb to be added liberally in cooking – preventative medicine at its best!

Parsley can also be chewed after eating garlic to freshen the breath.

Rosemary

Rosemary is steeped in folklore and has been burnt to ward off evil spirits in the past. Putting a sprig on the barbeque after cooking will ward off mosquitoes and night-time bugs.

Sage

Sage is a natural antiseptic and will aid in the healing of minor cuts and grazes. At certain times in history sage has been known as a cure-all, but it has always been recognised as an important healing herb. A cup of sage tea every day will not only blow away the cobwebs and make you feel good, it is also effective in reducing menopausal symptoms such as hot flushes.

Thyme

Thyme is another strong antiseptic and it is effective in treating minor wounds. It has been recognised as a soothing herb, and a pillow of thyme can aid in a restful night's sleep.

Thyme has expectorant properties and is an excellent herb to infuse and drink as a tea at the onset of a cold or cough. Pour boiling water over a few sprigs of thyme in a jug, cover and leave for five minutes. Strain into a cup or glass and add a spoonful of honey to taste.

FROM CHAPTER 5 – FRUITY TREATS

Berries

As well as providing great fresh food value, strawberries, blackberries, blackcurrants and raspberries can be preserved to add a touch of summer vitamins to the winter months. Preserve as much fruit as possible for the winter in the form of jams, juices, frozen pies, and so on.

Lemons

Keep bits of lemons to rub around sinks and over kitchen work surfaces. The lemon removes grease and cleans without the need for bathroom or kitchen products. Rinse over lightly after using.

FROM CHAPTER 6 – DELICIOUS BLOOMS

All edible flowers are perfect for garnishing everyday meals or celebration dinners. And any flowers can be used in arts and crafts. Get the kids involved and make pressed flower birthday cards for someone special. Or create a beautiful pressed flower picture and frame it.

Dandelions

The milky sap from a dandelion stem is a helpful cure for warts and verrucas. This is a remedy worth trying before you head off to the chemist. Simply dab the sap directly onto the affected area two or three times a day.

Marigolds

Marigold petals make a useful dye and are a good food colourant. Add a few petals to cooked rice as a saffron alternative.

Roses

Add rose petals to pot pourri mixtures for colour and scent.

CHAPTER 9

THE STORE CUPBOARD

There are a number of simple ways to store your well-earned crops from the garden, as well as a few more complicated methods.

BOTTLING

Bottling fruit and vegetables is a worthwhile storage method if you have the right equipment and do it properly. Bottling fruit and veg requires a certain amount of care as bacteria can enter the food. Temperatures must be met and sterilising bottles and sealing them is imperative.

There are several different methods for bottling foods. For each method, use undamaged fruit or vegetables and prepare them by washing, draining, and then peeling and/or slicing.

The quickest way to bottle is to use a pressure cooker, although the cooker must be able to maintain a low pressure throughout the process.

Alternatively you can use a large saucepan with a false bottom or a wire rack at the bottom, as jars will crack if they are in direct contact with the saucepan when it is over the heat. Jars with rubber seals and spring clips should be used to keep your foods preserved well. The most useful ones have a capacity of 1 lb (500 g) or 2 lb (1 kg). All jars must be sterilised before using. You'll also need a decent thermometer to check that the correct temperature is reached.

Pack the prepared cold fruit or vegetables into jars. Pour over water, brine or fruit syrup so that the liquid fills all the gaps. Water can be used with all foods but you may choose to use brine for vegetables and syrup for fruit as you prefer. Place the jars in a saucepan of cold water. The water should be brought to the boil slowly and simmered until the correct temperature has been reached. Alternatively jars can be packed with warm fruit and water and placed in hot water to reduce the cooking time.

Bottling can also be done in a very slow oven. The jars must not touch each other or the sides of the oven.

Different foods require different cooking times and temperatures to preserve them safely. Approximately 190.4°F or 88°C is the usual temperature required to bottle fruits and vegetables safely using a hot water saucepan method, although with a cold water process a slightly lower temperature will work. Cooking times vary between about 2 and 15 minutes, depending on the foods you are bottling. A pressure cooker will sort it all out in about one or two minutes. Check temperature and time charts for each type of food before processing. There is a very informative and useful section on the website www.allotment.org.uk – follow the information links.

Suitable foods for bottling

Most fruits and vegetables can be bottled or canned although some foods lose some of their colour and texture during the bottling process. Generally most fruits are very suitable for bottling, as long as they are used undamaged and prepared correctly. Some green vegetables will lose some colour and texture, but will stay perfectly edible.

PRESERVING

Although making jams, jellies and pickles is similar to bottling food, the process is less time consuming and, as you can make all sorts of jams and pickles, is far more fun than simply storing food in its original state. Most fruit and veg can be made into jams or pickles and there are only a few basic rules to follow for either preserving method.

Jams and jellies require sugar to preserve the fruit and generally pickled vegetables are preserved with vinegar.

Suitable foods for preserving

Soft fruits are perfect for making jams and jellies. See Chapter 5 for recipes for strawberry jam and others. Citrus fruits such as oranges and lemons can be made into marmalade, using the same basic principle as sweet fruit jams.

Apples and pears can be puréed and, after storing in jars, can be used to make pies and other dishes in the winter months. Apple purée or apple sauce can be served with a favourite roast pork dinner, or eaten as a dessert with ice cream. Children tend to like easy to eat foods and puréed fruit is a good way of getting them to eat a daily portion or two of fruit.

FREEZING

Freezing is probably the easiest and quickest way to preserve food, although not all foods will freeze and keep their texture and taste. With soft fruits, freezing quickly helps to keep the texture and flavour but inevitably some will be lost during freezing. One way round this is to make up whole dishes before freezing. For example a blackberry and apple pie will be more acceptable in its different texture than simply a bag of apples and blackberries.

Lay fruits, vegetables or herbs on trays and freeze quickly. Store in containers or bags and label before storing in the freezer.

Suitable foods for freezing

Most foods can be successfully frozen although fruit and veg with a high water content will dramatically change texture and, in some cases, colour, after freezing. Lettuce is very definitely a vegetable *not* to freeze, although, if frozen quickly, other leafy vegetables such as spinach will work reasonably well. Peas, beans, broccoli and cauliflower freeze successfully.

DRYING

Some food crops dry incredibly well, and it's a good idea to take advantage of this fact if you have storage space and lots of excess food from the garden. Always make sure food is properly dried before storing to avoid cross contamination or mould forming.

Suitable foods for drying

HERBS AND LEAFY VEGETABLES

Hang bunches of herbs, or single stems, in a dark dust-free place for up to a couple of weeks until completely dry. Some herbs will be dry enough in two or three days. Check regularly. Hang the herbs in paper bags to protect from dust and airborne mites. The bags will also collect any seeds or dried leaf that may fall from the stems or bunches. When completely dry, crumble and store the herbs in sealed glass jars and label. Keep the jars out of direct sunlight. Seeds can be kept for use in the kitchen or for planting next year.

Sprigs of herbs drying

Most vegetables can be dried using a home food dryer or in a slow oven. Vegetables should be blanched first to kill any bugs. Slice or cut vegetables and place in a muslin or cheesecloth bag and place in a saucepan of boiling water. Keep the water boiling for about five minutes. Remove the bag from the saucepan and place in a bowl of cold water for five minutes. (This seals in the vitamins and minerals.) Drain well then spread a single layer of prepared vegetables on a rack in a home dryer or dry in a fairly cool oven, as described opposite for dried tomatoes.

PEAS AND BEANS

Peas and beans are exceptionally good for drying. Dried peas used to be taken on long sea voyages many years ago and would keep the crew and passengers fed for months. Dried peas and beans are simple to prepare and, as far as possible, should be left on the plant until totally mature and dry. Otherwise lay them on trays in a warm dry place until all trace of moisture is gone before storing.

Make sure there are no holes in peas and beans before storing as this can indicate that worms are present. Rather than picking over individual peas or beans to check for worms, fill a bowl with water and put the peas or beans in

188

the water. The ones that float will have holes and should not be stored unless you are sure there is no worm left inside. These can be eaten but the worms will have eaten a lot of the goodness so try and store only the best, especially if you are likely to be keeping them for several months. They will keep almost indefinitely if prepared well and stored out of direct light in sealed jars.

MUSHROOMS
Mushrooms are a viable produce to dry. They can be strung together and hung over a range or radiator for a few days, then bagged and labelled before storing. Keep them out of direct light.

TOMATOES
Sun-dried tomatoes are a popular food but can be expensive to buy. Tomatoes can, however, be dried at home very successfully. Although they should be 'sun' dried, there is little chance of finding enough hours of sunshine in the UK at the end of the summer, but tomatoes can be dried successfully in a slow oven.

Cut tomatoes in half and place them cut side up on a baking sheet, leaving a little space between them. Put the tray in a very slow oven (Gas Mark ½, 250°F or 130°C) for an hour or two. Check every 30 minutes or so, and remove the tomatoes that are completely dry. If the tomatoes start to cook, leave the oven door ajar. At the end of this drying process, allow the tomatoes to cool completely and store in labelled bags or containers out of direct light. Sprinkle a little chopped basil, sea salt or even parmesan cheese if liked over the tomatoes before drying and store as above.

CHAPTER 10
GARDENING TIPS AND TRICKS

A little preparation goes a long way in the garden. Scattering the seed and hoping for the best won't produce the results you want. If you get to know your garden – the hot spots, the wet spots and any drafty areas – you can accommodate your plants well and get great results. Plants need water, light and air to thrive. Some need more of one and less of another, which is why good preparation will bring the best results as well as a garden that takes less time and effort in the long run to maintain.

Any neglected plants can be brought back to life with a little care and attention. Old rose trees and shrubs will benefit from a heavy pruning. Any plants that look well past their use-by date or don't fit in with your garden plans have to go. Dig them up and put them on the compost heap. Any diseased plants should be burned.

Are there areas of the garden that are magnets for local cats or other animals? A couple of paving slabs over a sandy area will put the local cat's bathroom out of action. Keeping grass cut short will also deter cats and other wildlife from damaging your plants. Very fine soil can be mulched until the feline population gets the message. If cats are a nuisance in your garden, make sure you protect seeds with a cloche or cover straight after sowing.

PLANNING

Most plants thrive in sunlight, so the best place to put your shed will be in a shady spot in the garden. Don't waste a sunny position. Make sure you can clear right around the shed so that hedgerows or stray brambles don't grow over it.

The rest of the garden can be broken up with various beds, rockeries, water features, seating areas and children's play areas. Draw a plan of your garden. It doesn't have to be to scale, although a little precision is always useful!

Decide where your priorities lie in the garden. Consider some of these ideas:

- **Seating** can be placed among the herb beds or rose garden as well as on the patio. Consider a garden arbour with a seat. Grapes or other climbing vines can be grown over them, making the most of the space. Or build a bench around a tree – remember to allow room for the tree to grow though.

- **Containers of herbs and flowers** grace a patio and can also draw the eye to features around the garden. A large container of marigolds next to the back door brightens up the house and a container of flowering herbs will enhance a water feature.

- **Vegetable beds** in a *le potager* design makes the whole vegetable gardening thing seem a lot less overwhelming. Simply create small square beds where you can grow vegetables with herbs around the edges. Get creative with this idea. Bright green herbs around a bed of red cabbage looks stunning, for example.

Containers of herbs growing

- **Raised beds** need a lot less maintenance than a regular vegetable patch. They have to be narrow enough to reach the middle from both sides and then once dug over thoroughly, won't need digging again for a few years. These beds can be permanent and have brick or wooden sides, creating a feature of themselves in your garden. Higher beds are also useful for the physically challenged as they require less bending over or kneeling.

- **Flowers and herbs** can be mixed in with vegetable and fruit crops as long as they don't overcrowd. Herbs are good plants to grow with your vegetables as many of them are strong smelling and deter pests from vegetable crops. Flowers will encourage pollinating bees to your garden.

- A **water feature** is sometimes considered to be a luxury but a pond will encourage wildlife to your garden. Frogs and toads live happily in a lush vegetable garden with a pond nearby and they are the best organic slug repellent around. Ponds and water features also attract children, providing a perfect way to get them away from the latest computer game!

- A **compost heap** is essential if you are going to take your gardening seriously. Either build it or buy one of the composting tumblers available in big garden centres or suppliers. Composting rotten fruit and vegetables and peelings creates rich soil you can use every year to plant seedlings or container plants. This really is recycling at its best. Dig out the bottom of your compost heap once a year and sieve the soil before using it. A simple garden sieve can be made by stretching a piece of chicken wire across an old bottomless saucepan or strong bucket. A compost heap needs to be kept warm but it also needs air to break down the vegetation. Leave gaps in the sides for air and cover the top after adding composting material.

TOOLS

Once you have decided what you are doing and where everything is going, a few tools will come in handy. You won't need everything to begin with and quality is better than quantity every time when it comes to garden tools. Cheap tools can buckle and cause damage to your plants as well as to you.

To get your fruit, vegetable, herb or flowerbed started, you will need to buy:

- A **spade and fork** for digging over, breaking up the ground and edging. Both tools must be the right height for you to use them. Handle them in the shop before you buy. Make sure you don't have to lean over the handle or that it isn't too long for you. Their weight is also important. If you can hardly lift it in the shop, you definitely won't be able to lift it when it's full of wet soil. A sharp edge on your spade is useful for defining your beds, which in turn helps to keep weeds from straying into them.

- A **rake and a hoe** are essential for breaking up the ground and levelling off. Rakes are also useful for dragging stones from the surface of the soil, so make sure it is strong. A hoe should be fairly sharp for cutting through soil. Both tools must be the right height and weight as above.

- A **hand trowel and watering can** are the only hand tools you will need to begin gardening. You can add more later as and when they are needed. The trowel must be strong and the watering can should have a rosette attachment. Make sure the can isn't too heavy for you; when it's full of water it will be a lot heavier!

For seed sowers a few extra bits and pieces are needed, although alternatives can be found:

POTS

- Plastic green or black pots can be bought in most garden suppliers and there are often biodegradable alternatives.

- Save yoghurt and dessert pots, wash and dry them thoroughly then carefully punch holes in the bottom for drainage. Don't use pots without holes as seeds will rot.

- Inner cardboard tubes from kitchen or toilet rolls make ideal seed starters. The whole tube or roll can be planted as they are biodegradable and, although they are made of card, they last a while and are ideal for seeds that are fairly quick to germinate such as tomatoes, lettuces and most other everyday vegetables.

- Make pots from newspaper, using a specially designed pot maker, available in larger garden centres.

SEED TRAYS

- Buy a few seed trays from a garden centre but don't buy flimsy trays as they tend to crack and break easily.

- Old paint roller trays are a good alternative to bought seed trays. Make sure all paint is thoroughly washed away before filling with compost. Punch holes in the bottom for drainage.

- Deep silver foil baking dishes can also be used. They should be rinsed after using and holes punched in the bottom. The very shallow trays aren't really deep enough to germinate most seeds, although they are perfect for mustard and cress.

ROW MARKERS

- Plastic labels can be bought from garden suppliers as well as the right type of marker to write on them.

- Get the kids making drinking-straw flags for your pot markers. Sellotape or glue a plain piece of paper around one end of a drinking straw. Leave enough space to write on. Cut some straws in half for seed tray markers.

- Use wooden lolly sticks, or collect small twigs on your next woodland walk.

OTHER HELPFUL ODDS AND ENDS

- A dry box is useful for keeping your seeds in before sowing.

- Keep a pen available to label your plants and a journal if you are keeping one.

- A pair of gardening gloves saves a lot of wear and tear on your hands and nails.

- An old spoon or fork from the cutlery drawer can be useful for transplanting small plants.

SOIL PREPARATION

Drainage

It's worth doing a little research into the condition of the soil in your garden, although we don't have to get too technical. Generally it's important to have well-drained soil. There are very few plants that will survive in waterlogged soil so that's the first check to make. Whatever you are planning to grow, whether it's fruit, vegetables herbs or flowers, you will need well-drained soil.

- Incorporate some fine gravel or sand to alleviate any drainage problems.

- Consider building raised beds if the ground is very badly drained.

- Or use containers to plant your crops.

Nutrients

Generally fruit and vegetables will need fairly well-nourished soil. Some herbs and a few fruits and veg will tolerate poor soil but in general, the more nutrients in the soil, the more your vegetables will thrive. And of course the more nutritious your vegetables, the better for you.

- Dig in some well-rotted manure or rich compost into the soil before planting.

- For root crops, it's advisable to dig the fertilisers into the ground during the previous autumn. Un-rotted material will cause root crops to 'fork' and also may be too rich for some young plants.

Digging over

Once the soil is in the condition you are happy with, it will need digging over if you haven't done so already. Don't over-do the digging. It's tempting on the first sunny day of the year to go out there and dig a whole bed over in one day but that usually results in an aching back and being out of action for a week or two.

Take it a little at a time. Even if you only dig over a square metre a day, it's good enough. It's also much better for the spirit as well as the body. If you plan to dig over only a small part of the large vegetable patch, it doesn't seem like a chore.

Dig as deep as you can the first time, especially if the ground hasn't been used for a while. Remove large stones, non-organic debris and any perennial weeds.

Compost the weeds, keep the stones for drainage and edging later on and dispose of any other rubbish. Keep the area tidied as you go along.

When the bed has been dug over, rake to a fine tilth and let it rest. Some gardeners like to cover the area with black plastic or other materials to discourage weeds. If you cover the ground, remove the covering a week or two before planting to aerate the soil. Break up the surface with a hoe if necessary.

Mulch

A mulch is useful in the winter to prevent frost damage. It also keeps the weeds down during the summer and helps to keep moisture in. Use grass clippings, straw or other organic materials. Never mulch too close to your plants or they will suffocate. Lay your mulching material around the plants to cover the soil. It only needs to be a few centimetres deep.

MAINTENANCE

If possible, a garden should be maintained on a daily basis. With bad weather and short days this is not always possible. During the winter months, try and do some of the maintenance there isn't time for in the summer. For example, fixing garden fences, catches on gates, shed doors that won't close. Tidying up these little jobs in the winter makes the spring and summer seasons in the garden so much easier and more enjoyable.

Pruning can also be done during the autumn to early spring. Cut back your fruit bushes, roses, trees and other shrubs. A few minutes spent here and there will provide much better crops or blooms the following year.

Plant trees and other hardy shrubs in the autumn to settle in before the following spring.

Clover lawns

Lawn specialists get frustrated with clover growing in the lawn as it is considered to be a weed. However, clover stays green all year and doesn't need cutting as often as grass does. It also encourage bees to your garden, so factor this in if you have children as bare feet could get stung.

Raised beds

As mentioned before, raised beds really do take the hard work out of spring planting. Double dig your bed in the first year and make sure it's not too wide so that you can reach to the middle from both sides. Don't walk over the bed once dug and you will only need to gently fork it over the following spring before planting.

Plants can be placed closer together in a raised bed, giving you more available growing space.

Paved areas

A few paving slabs can be useful in the garden. Be adventurous and place one in the middle of a flowerbed to make a plinth for a particularly attractive container full of herbs. Paving slabs are also useful for covering sandy areas, preventing local cats using your garden as their public convenience.

THEMES

Themed gardens need a little more planning but the effect can be spectacular.

- **Meadow and wildlife gardens** are becoming very popular but if you want to grow vegetables alongside you may have a lot of weeding to do. Consider growing meadow flowers in a small part of your garden next to a path to prevent trailing plants taking over. Bees will be attracted to a wildlife garden and help to pollinate your vegetables.

Butterfly

- A **butterfly garden** planted out with flowers that particularly attract butterflies is a popular and fairly simple theme to create, but again remember the veggies. Cabbage white butterflies let loose on your cabbages will lay eggs on the underside of the leaves and, if not spotted in time, the resulting caterpillars can demolish crops almost overnight.

- **Colours** can be used as a theme – blue flowers in the spring, yellow in the summer and so on. Become an expert flower grower and you will be sought after in your area. Scan a few catalogues for ideas. There are some wonderfully coloured hybrid blooms on the market these days. Not all flowers are annual but bulbs, such as tulips, daffodils and crocuses, will last for many years and often reproduce themselves, making your display bigger and better every year.

- **Rose gardens** have always been a gardener's delight and can be added to every year. From very tiny tea roses to large rambling dog roses, the choice is huge. Again browse a few catalogues to see what's available and what will suit your garden. Climbing roses brighten up a bare brick wall over a few growing seasons and will last for many years.

- Your garden could be given over completely to growing **herbs**. Herbs can be grown in containers and are useful and aromatic plants to grow in your garden. Herbs are a subject in themselves and can provide not only wonderful flavourings for food but also many can be used as alternative medicines and even cosmetics. See Chapter 4 on herbs for more ideas.

- **Water features** can be stunning and soothing, as any feng shui enthusiast will tell you. A small courtyard will be transformed with a water feature and a few containers of herbs. Let your imagination loose on this one. Create a rock garden or a rockery and have water trickling over the rocks into a pond. Fish are good entertainment for the kids and you could grow some excellent watercress in the running water. Features like this will take a certain amount of planning and budget should be considered. Look around before you buy. You may find something that suits your space even better than your original idea.

Any outdoor space is an extension of your home and, with a little attention, it will delight and inspire everyone. Give it some thought before you begin. Be realistic about how much time, effort and money you are prepared to invest.

Taking on too much too soon in a garden becomes overwhelming and all too easily gets neglected. If you are facing a huge task, take it on a little at a time. Decide to get a vegetable bed going the first year, adding other features in subsequent years, as and when you have the time available.

Gardens are there to grow and your garden should always be 'a work in progress' and never actually finished!

RESOURCES AND FURTHER READING

MORE TITLES BY LINDA GRAY

Grow Your Own Pharmacy (Findhorn Press)

Granny's Book of Good Old Fashioned Common Sense (Black & White Publishing)

Herb Gardening (Crowood Press)

WEBSITES

Gardening and plants

www.flower-and-garden-tips.com

www.bbc.co.uk/gardening

www.botanical.com

www.gardenguides.com

www.garden.org (National Gardening Association)

Healthy living

www.5aday.nhs.uk

www.bbc.co.uk/health/healthy_living

www.nutrition.org.uk (British Nutrition Foundation)

www.thinkvegetables.co.uk

FURTHER READING

The Practical Gardening Encyclopaedia (Colour Library)

Complete Garden Manual (Collins)

INDEX